"This collection of c⸏ hopeful, and inspired. Th⸏ ⸏⸏⸏⸏⸏⸏, ⸏⸏⸏⸏⸏⸏⸏⸏⸏, ⸏⸏⸏ ⸏⸏⸏- severance these women exemplify moved me to tears, and healed parts of my soul that were unknowingly hurting. I'm grateful for their tangible tools and takeaways. Everyone can learn from these powerful voices who struggled in silence, and sang anyhow."

-Krysta Lee, actor, author of
Mama's Gotta Work and *Women Let's Rise*
www.KrystaLee.com | @KrystaLee111

"Angel Kibble, [chapter 11] you have the gift of telling your story in a way that just connects with the people that need to hear this. I was glued to your words feeling everything you went through and even connecting with you through my own experiences of abuse. The way you so elegantly write the twists and turns makes the reader (me) realize that we can decide what is no longer our story and we can rewrite a new chapter. We are in control. Thank you for sharing such vulnerability. You are a voice meant to help many! WoW!"

-Bruno Guévremont, Bell Let's Talk Ambassador,
Invictus Games 2016 Team Canada Captain

"*She's No Longer Silent* helped me to reevaluate myself and the negative relationships I was in. This book bettered my life. Authors Kiki Carr and Lori Williamson are a wealth of knowledge. Charleyne Oulton, Sasha Rose, and Angel Kibble are strong story tellers. Mandy Karpoff's unique writing style is gripping."

-Ky-Lee Hanson, award winning publisher,
human rights advocate, @gbrpublishing

"Kady's [chapter 13] enthusiasm for life is second only to her passionate desire to share her wisdom garnered from her personal and professional experiences. Her masterful use of tools and resources to continue to support and guide herself and others to overcome 'fear when it rears its ugly head' is uplifting and commendable."

-Anna Pavan, Retired Executive Director of an agency that supports women and children

"Griping, Powerful, and Raw. Your heart bleeds, savouring each story of strength, loss, fight, triumph and survival. *She's No Longer Silent* is a tribute to the wonderment that is to be a Woman. I couldn't put it down and I'm waiting for my heart to stop pounding so I can pick it back up and read it again."

-Habiba Jessica Zaman, Therapist

She's No Longer Silent

Healing after mental health trauma, sexual abuse, and experiencing injustice.

Charleyne Oulton, Kiki Carr, Sasha Rose,
Angel Kibble, Nicole Taylor Eby, Katryna Rose,
Violaine Pigeon, Lori Williamson, Mlle Elizabeth Ann,
Kady Romagnuolo, Whitney Stout, Stephanie Reid,
Nicole Thomas, Cassaundra Noyes, Lindsay Whitham,
Mandy Karpoff, Eldyka Simpson

GOLDEN BRICK ROAD
PUBLISHING HOUSE

Published in Canada, for Global Distribution by Golden Brick Road Publishing House Inc.

www.goldenbrickroad.pub

For more information email: kylee@gbrph.ca

ISBN: 9781988736754

To order additional copies of this book: orders@gbrph.ca

TABLE OF CONTENTS

SECTION ONE

SECTION TWO

SECTION THREE

TO THE READER:

A memoir is one's written personal experience. It is a book of memory. And memory is fallible and unreliable. This book is, therefore, an inaccurate account. It should be read as a story. We have done our best to tell our stories honestly, through the dark glass of hindsight. This book reflects our present recollections of what we lived through. Not only were these lived experiences from deep in our past, they have the ability to cause deep emotional Upheaval. Memories resurfaced, and they are among the stories that we are recounting herein. Resurfaced memories are, too, not infallibly accurate.

So, why write a memoir at all?

To tell stories to protect the marginalized. Specifically, to help women who are mentally and emotionally imprisoned. This memoir is not meant to exact retribution against anyone, which is why names are avoided or have been changed. We share our experiences, to help others in their struggle. All the names, places, and details have been changed to protect actual individuals, living and dead. We have also changed or omitted identifying characteristics and details such as physical properties, and places of residence. Further, events have been compressed and statements have been recreated, as in any story. A story is not reality. A story can be read in one sitting, or read and re-read over a lifetime. This story is not a chronology of events to be used to defame anyone, or to litigate anything.

This story is meant to give solace to those who face adversity alone. People can have different memories of events. In these stories, we share what happened to us, from our individual point of view. It should be read as an honest account, but not a specific one, except to us. There is no malice in our hearts, and no desire to identify anyone. The conversations in the book all come from our recollections, and are not written to represent word-for-word transcripts. Rather, retold in a way to evoke the feeling and meaning of what was said in those instances, as recalled, albeit fallibly.

The reader should know, however, all stories can be corroborated by witnesses, or other evidence. This is our assurance to the reader that they are truly not alone. We share our experiences and struggles to serve as a safe harbour to anyone. This book is intended for good. This is our narrative memory. And memory is fallible and unreliable.

If you are facing any kind of stress, harassment, or feelings of hopelessness, do not wait another moment to reach out for help.

* * * DISCLAIMER * * *

This book contains stories with adult content and language that may be offensive to some readers. Recommended for mature audiences and content may be triggering for some readers.

Subject matter includes suicide, violence, sexual abuse, and mature content.

If you are in immediate danger or fear for your safety, please call 9-1-1.

PREFACE

Charleyne Oulton

You are enough.
You are good enough.
You are smart enough.
You are strong enough.
You are beautiful enough.
You are kind enough.
You are brave enough.
You are and always will be enough.

In North America, one in four will face a mental health problem in any given year;[1] someone is sexually assaulted every seventy-three seconds;[2] and one in three women experience some physical violence by an intimate partner. On a typical day, there are more than 20,000 phone calls placed to domestic violence hotlines.[3] In Canada, 40% of Canadian workers have experienced bullying on a weekly basis.[4] In 2019, personality disorders affected between 6% and 15% of the North American population.[5]

She's No Longer Silent, in its rare honesty and intimate detail, is both an open wound and a salve. Our quietest cries to our loudest scream. These words and experiences are sadly all too relatable for many women. We are sharing both our vulnerability and our immense strength. Our growth and our pain.

Trauma and mental illness can cause unseen pain and psychological distress leaving invisible wounds that are harder to detect,

1   "Mood Disorders Society of Canada's Quick Facts: Mental Health & Addictions in Canada," Mood Disorders Society of Canada, booklet dated 2019, https://mdsc.ca/edu/quick-facts-on-mental-illness-addiction-in-canada/
2   "Statistics on Violence Against Women in BC," Ending Violence Association of BC, 2019 https://endingviolence.org/prevention-programs/be-more-than-a-bystander/be-more-than-a-bystander-statistics/
3   "Family Violence in Canada: A Statistical Profile, 2018," Statistics Canada, booklet dated 2019, https://www150.statcan.gc.ca/n1/en/pub/85-002-x/2019001/article/00018-eng.pdf?st=vvHbzB8i.
4   "Canadian Bullying Statistics," Canadian Institutes of Health Research, last modified September 28, 2012, https://cihr-irsc.gc.ca/e/45838.html
5   "Section F-Personality Disorders," Statistics Canada, last modified November 27, 2015, https://www150.statcan.gc.ca/n1/pub/82-619-m/2012004/sections/sectionf-eng.htm

understand, and heal from than many bodily injuries. Victims may be targeted on the basis of their sex, gender, race, ethnicity, religion, sexual orientation, gender identity, physical appearance, or disability. Survivors may have intense negative feelings long after their suffering has ended. Many suffer with anxiety, flashbacks, depression, trust issues, and lack of healthy boundaries. The cure to women's lack of empowerment is speaking out. *She's No Longer Silent* is a brave beginning. We can learn from one another and help each other. Healing *can* come after pain.

We want you to know, from our experiences, that finding a safe place to take the time and space you need is crucial to healing. If you feel trapped, alone, or terrified, our stories are here to remind you how worthy, loved, and valuable you truly are. Your feelings are valid and important. We know from experience how it feels to suffer silently. Our stories collectively are intended to offer support to all without question and without judgement. We share our struggles and the pain we have lived through, including the isolation and shame we endured. We hope you can learn and gain strength from our experiences.

Our individual stories collectively illustrate a culture biased to having victims remain silent. She's No Longer Silent aims to forever transform the way society thinks about mental complexes, personality disorders, injustice, and abuse. It challenges our beliefs about what we can say, think, and do.

This is where we find our voices together. Together, as women, we are united in breaking the silence and stigmas of today's society.

Mental illness, trauma, and injustice can
happen to anyone; it does not discriminate.

INTRODUCTION

Kiki Carr

Situations where I was silent or was expected to be silent:
When tormentors dressed as victims.
When I discovered my mental illness.
When a seemingly close friend was stealthily bullying me.
When someone I knew was being abused.
When someone I knew had an eating disorder.
When someone needed a person to stand up for them.
When the crowd had a mob mentality.

Situations where being silent seemed better:
People around me didn't want conflict.
It was more convenient for everyone else.
Rocking the boat made others uncomfortable.
If I spoke up, they would paint me as the troublemaker or the bully.
It would challenge the status quo.
The finger would be pointed at me instead of the issue needing resolution.
Outing a victim and taking their power from them.
I would become the target and my voice was not heard.
The victim gets targeted and blamed.
When you speak out, your power echoes.
When you speak your truth, your strength ignites.

If using our voices can alter realities, then why is it so difficult for many of us?

Everyone has a story, a message to share, and a journey to recount. But sometimes we are silenced. In this silence, a slow moving blanket of suffering wraps itself around us. The silencing comes swift and unseen, swiping our souls with darkness.

The women in this book have done what many feel is impossible. They have taken one step forward in reclaiming what has always been theirs, their voice. The journeys within *She's No Longer Silent* are being recounted as a symbol of strength and resilience toward an empowered life. Our traumas do not define us, but are a part of our ever evolving stories. It all started with one word, one step, and one goal to take back their lives to show you that you can too. The darkness that held us from healing was the silent shackles that kept us stranded and alone. The sound of our voices, big or small, is the catalyst we all used to finally break the chains that bound us.

This book is for those who cannot speak when they need it most. We are a guiding light, a vessel, and advocates for people's rights. We have been where many have been—maybe you have been too—we are here to share that there is beauty in the unfolding. With many stories and journeys of silence being shared throughout, it's important to ask yourself if you are ready to hear and read the stories that could be triggering. Make sure you are in a mindset that will allow the love and growth to pour from the words, into your heart. Every person will read this book and be affected differently, with real emotions and real reactions. Notice these emotions and ask yourself: What are you feeling? Where in your body do you feel this emotion? Why do you think you feel it? How can you support yourself through? What do you need?

We may not know your specific story and we may not have the exact answers for you, but the stories in this book are written with love for you to discover your individual needs. This book is a safe space for you to explore in the way that feels right to you.

SECTION ONE

Not All Wounds are Visible: Give Yourself Credit for the Days You Made It When You Thought You Couldn't

When someone truly cares about you, they make an effort, not an excuse.

FEATURING

Crystal Hardy Zongwe Binesikwe
Katryna Rose
Nicole Thomas
Nicole Taylor Eby
Cassaundra Noyes
Violaine Pigeon

Dear Self,
I know you are doing
the best you can.
I believe in you.
Keep going.

-Love, ME
xox.

Daughters of Four Generations

Crystal Hardy Zongwe Binesikwe

Violet was a daughter.
She was a mother of four;
She always wanted sons;
She had one daughter who loved her.
She loved her children but could not show it;
She hurt her daughter.
Her daughter struggled and could not forgive her.

Ruby was a daughter.
She was a mother of three;
She wanted children but she was very young;
She had two daughters that loved her.
She loved her children but could not show it;
She was hurt by others and continued to struggle.

Crystal is a daughter.
She is a mother of two;
She always wanted children;
She has one daughter that loves her.
She loves her children and shows them every day.
She was hurt as a child but forgave to
move forward;
She will never hurt her children;
Her children will not struggle.

Evelyn is a daughter.
She is not yet a mother;
She is still a child.
One day she may have children that will love her;
She will love her children and show them
every day.

She has never been hurt;
She has never struggled, and neither will
her children.

Struggle no more, future daughters.

CHAPTER ONE

I Am a Master of Survival, Thanks to My Mental Illness

"Sometimes not knowing the 'why' is what helps us discover the 'how'."

KATRYNA ROSE

KATRYNA ROSE

Katryna is a passionate writer who began her journey with pen and paper when she was just eight years old. The death of her father inspired her to start writing, and she hasn't stopped since. Poetry is at the top of her list of favorite writing styles, and a close second is writing music. Katryna is a proud mother of two beautiful girls: Kashlyn (six) and Cannyn (six months).

From a very young age, Katryna dreamed of working with and educating young children. She achieved that goal and started educating when she was twenty-three years old. She worked for multiple daycares and two school boards before being assaulted at work, which changed her life entirely. She became both physically and mentally disabled, and was diagnosed with a panic disorder, with agoraphobia, and PTSD when she was just twenty-nine years old. The assault she experienced at work triggered her existing circumstantial depression and anxiety into an unpredictable disorder and illness. After years of suffering, Katryna became strong enough to share her experiences with others (on her good days), and became a strong advocate in the mental health community. Some of her best work has come from her hardships. She is determined to help stop the stigma surrounding mental illness. Thanks to her inspiration, determination, and love for writing, Katryna was destined to cross paths with Golden Brick Road Publishing.

www.katrynarose.com

ig: @katrynarose11 | f: @katryna.arseneau | li: @Katryna Rose

t: @KatrynaRose11

Sometimes, life graces us with gifts. These gifts can come in the form of a smile, a kind gesture, or shared knowledge (among many other things).

I was a happy, outgoing, brave little girl who loved to be outside. Nature always calmed me. To this day, if I feel closed up or I need a release, a simple walk through the forest or along the beach can help bring me back. The feeling of the sand between my toes and the sludge of muddy sand water makes me feel alive, as does the sound of crunching, dried-up leaves that have fallen from their giant homes in the forest. Nature always understood me, always accepted me, no matter what state I was in, no matter where I lived, no matter what point I was at in my life.

I grew up on a farm in Alberton, Ontario, Canada. We had ducks, rabbits, a Canadian goose (a rescue), and a slew of other animals. My parents brought me up to respect all walks of life and to help any creature in need. I believe that learning those qualities so young helped shape me into the woman I am today. I believe that we all have gifts to share, and we always have time to help others. The hardest part was learning that the first person I had to help was myself. If I could give you any advice at all. I would tell you to go do something just for you. Get up each morning and do something that makes your heart smile. No matter how big or small- gifting yourself with purposeful happiness can help you along the path to healing. And it's just plain and simply good for the soul.

My father passed away from brain cancer when I was eight years old. I saw it all: the appointments, treatments, tubes, doctors, stitches, staples, hair loss, seizures, and eventually the breakdown of a man whom I believed to be a real-life superhero. I can say that I truly understand what it means to have a broken heart. My depression started so young that I have a hard time remembering myself before my father passed away. I've had anxiety since I can remember, and my first memory of worrying is when I was about five years of age. I worried about my father dying, I worried about my future without him, and I worried about him worrying about me.

I became the child who was closed off and socially awkward; I was just kind of "there." I remember a period of time when I didn't want to leave my room after he passed away (a phase that lasted one year or so). I would pile all of my stuffed animals in my closet and sit in there with them, as though surrounding myself with matted fur and plastic eyes would somehow make me feel better. I would stay in my closet for hours and just think, analyze, or sleep. Sometimes I could hear my mother call for me, but I didn't make a peep. I would hear my door creak open as she slowly pushed her way in to look for me. I could hear her voice echo as she called my name and turned to walk back down the hallway. Hours would pass as the darkness stayed still. The darkness helped me escape my reality, and I was safe within that emptiness. It didn't hurt as much as real life did. I felt like I was stuck in between life and death.

I so eagerly wanted to be with my father, yet I didn't want to miss my siblings and mother. I missed him so desperately, I needed him still, I was lost without him. I started my fatherless journey so lost and confused.

At school, I didn't go out of my way to make friends anymore. Avoiding anyone and anything became a habit of mine; my personality had completely changed. My heart was broken and there was no way to fix it, unless someone could bring my dad back. I learned that avoiding social situations made me feel more comfortable, and it helped to get me through a little longer. If I noticed my friends grouping at the end of the hall, I would turn direction and head the opposite way. When sitting alone during recess, I would ignore anyone who called out my name unless they walked right up to me and I had no other way to escape. I did my best not to stand out and avoided as much as I could.

At family gatherings, I began to sneak out at the end, instead of taking the time to say goodbye to each of my family members. Saying goodbye was now something I was no longer willing to do. My smile was never as big as it was prior to his passing. I lost excitement for life for some time. I didn't want to go on without him and I felt sick to my stomach if I thought about it for too long. I submerged myself into writing and music. It became my therapy, and I can say with 100% certainty that it saved my life. Without the ability to write how I felt onto paper; my pain would have eaten me alive very slowly.

If it weren't for the love I have for my family, I know I would not have survived the pain I felt. Shortly after my father passed away, my mother booked an appointment for me to speak with a professional. She knew she was losing me and could see that I needed help. I will never forget that day. A grown man sat across from me, looked me straight in the eye, and asked me how I was feeling. If I had been some smart-ass kid, I probably would have laughed in his face. But I wasn't that. I was a very intelligent little girl, and wise beyond my years. And so I looked down and didn't say a word. I thought to myself, *If this adult is asking how I am feeling, it means he has absolutely no clue how this feels.* I could tell by the look on his face and the pen dancing between his fingers that my words would do no justice. Whatever book he had read about understanding a child losing a parent, could not have educated him enough to help me. I understood this and in that moment, I had never felt so alone. That was the extent of the therapy I received after my father passed away. Today, my mother says she never would have taken me if she could have foreseen my experience (but at the time, she had no idea how to help me). Looking back now, if I had been the adult in the situation, I would have found some sort of brother/sister club and given myself the opportunity to speak with other kids who felt the same way, or connected me with an adult who had experienced a similar situation when they were younger. I would never recommend having a child speak to someone who hasn't lived through this situation. In fact, I still wish to this day that someone had better prepared me to see my father's dead body. At his funeral I felt excited to see him again. I ran up to his coffin and grabbed his hand. It shocked me and I pulled my hand away. No one told me he would be cold. No one told me he would look different. He had two days of service before we went to his burial. I was content playing in a room with a new toy while people came to pay their respects. I wasn't upset until I had to leave him for the last time. My mother had to pull me from the parlour as I grabbed any wall or door frame possible to stay. I didn't want to leave him. To me, it was my dad laying in that coffin. Dead or not.

Puberty also started when I was eight years old, a month or so after my father passed away. I believe that my heart was so broken and my body so stressed that it jump-started puberty. I hid my period for days. I thought I was dying, just like my father had. At eight years old, I had no clue what a period was, and I thought it was best to keep it to myself and not tell my mother. After a few days, she found my stash of bloodied underwear and approached me with the conversation. To this day, I have not met anyone else who started puberty so young. I grew up too fast, and I learned so much in such a short amount of time. I was definitely wise beyond my years, and it was all due to the trauma of my childhood. Cancer forced me to grow up; I didn't have a choice. I understood what death was and I understood that life could be taken at any moment. I learned to say "I love you" as often as possible to the people I loved. It was around this time that a phobia started. Prior to my father's death, coming across a dead animal, or carcass did not bother me. After his passing I could not go anywhere near such a thing. If a pet died in our home (a hamster or bird), I would stay in my room until I knew the dead body was gone. I needed constant reassurance that the animal was gone, and I wouldn't come anywhere near it. When I walked on the sidewalks, I would look as far ahead as possible, to avoid any road kill. If ever there was something in sight, I would have to cross the road and tell myself there was nothing there, over and over, so I could pass it. I have that phobia to this day.

My teenage years weren't much better. My father's family did not come to see us anymore, and so I lost them, too. They chalked it up to something along the lines of "they were too upset from his dying wishes." My father had chosen to live his last moments at home surrounded by loved ones. He welcomed his closest family and friends whom he knew would help him be stress-free during those times. However, his mother had her own feelings about how he wanted to pass away. As a result, he distanced himself from her, and told her that if she could not support and accept his last wishes for peace at home, she would not be welcome. After my father passed away, his family chose not to see us anymore. They stopped calling. Birthday cards stopped coming. Years passed, and eventually I stopped asking to see them. At some point I accepted the fact that I was no longer wanted by them, and I buried my feelings about that very deep. Abandonment was extremely hard for me. Up until they exited my life, we were at their house nearly every Sunday of every week. I did not understand why they didn't want me anymore. I didn't understand why I wasn't worth them trying to see me (or talk to me) anymore.

Within a year and a half from the time my father died, my mother was remarried and pregnant with her new husband. From the second my stepfather came into our lives, we would never be the same. He was an abusive man who forever changed the person I was destined to be. He wasn't who we thought he was. My mother wasn't who she used to be. She didn't stand up to him or his abuse, and often I was the one who had to do it. It was difficult and sad, and I resented my mother for it for some time. I was abused in so many different ways. I was so vulnerable at that point in my life. Out of respect for my baby sister, I am choosing not to share anything more about him, but I will say that she (my baby sister) was the only good thing that came out of that relationship (and she means the world to me).

After their divorce, we moved from our beautiful home that my parents had built together, to a small town called Dundas, Ontario. Life there was a very different experience. And for the first time in a long time, it was a good one, although I fought the change at first. Initially I was so scared to leave the home where my father had passed, and where the old me lived. That was the home where all my memories were, both good and bad. Our new home was a fresh start for us though, and it was a good thing. For a second, I had a fresh start in life. For the first time since my father passed away, I felt like this opportunity would be what I needed to be happy again, and I saw a change in my mom. She smiled more and I could tell she was excited for this new chapter too.

My mother moved us to Dundas to get away from her ex-husband, but unfortunately he worked his way back in, and intoxicated our lives for a couple more years. During this time, I wasn't home as often as I should have been. I eventually ran away to my boyfriend's house. I spent the rest of my teenage years split between Dundas and my grandparents' house in Flamborough, Ontario.

I seemed to find abuse in every relationship I entered. I believe this stemmed from the abuse I endured as a child and teen. I had become used to it and so it was my normal. So many people had no idea how bad the abuse was; it was like a dark secret that filled up every inch of our home. I hated it and I hated him, and hate was what fuelled me for some time. I began to change again, just as I had after my father's death, but this time everything was even darker. I began to dress in all black, I dyed my hair dark, and I started to cover my pain up with drugs and alcohol—and I've overdosed on all of them. You name it, I've done it. While this is something I will never be proud of, it is a part of me and I can't change it. This is also something I feel is necessary to share. Don't ever be ashamed of what got you through a hard time. The fact that you are here is something to celebrate. So very often mental illness and drug abuse go hand-in-hand. We use one to cover up the pain of the other. It is nothing to feel ashamed about.

I was looking for an escape any way I could find it. I started cutting myself, I started getting body piercings, and I even got my first tattoo when I was just fourteen years old. I had my father's name (Tony) tattooed on my neck. There he stayed, in between my head and my heart, forever. I began to crave the feeling and sensation of physical pain. It drowned out the noise of my emotional pain, and for those moments, I was free. I became addicted to tattoos, piercings, and other forms of physical pain. The sensation became a portal to release my pain. Physical pain was something I needed to keep above my emotional pain. As long as I felt physical pain, I didn't have to deal with the emotional stuff.

These patterns of abuse and self-abuse continued for years. I stayed in a relationship for much longer than I should have; it ended with the left side of my face becoming paralyzed for six weeks. I was beaten up so badly that I blacked out. It felt as though I hovered above myself until the feeling of droplets brought me back to consciousness. I thought it had started to rain; I didn't realize it was my own blood spewing from my face until moments later. If my partner had hit me one more time, the bone that is one millimeter from my brain would have killed me. The surgeon said I was very lucky to be alive, but at the time, I wasn't sure that I agreed. In fact, I went to my friend's house that night, and stayed with him for a couple of days. I knew my face was broken in multiple places. That didn't stop me from doing drugs once more before I went home, and to the hospital for help (and surgery).

At my darkest of times, I attempted suicide because I believed it was the only way to escape my emotional pain. I felt like a burden to those I love (which couldn't have been any further from the truth). Instead, my family stayed by my side, and I am forever grateful for the strength they gave me to get through those times.

So when I say I understand, believe me, I do. And here's the good part: life gets better. At some point, I came to understand that each and every hard time was in fact a gift in disguise. I learned from each and every one of those incidents, and having the knowledge that came from those experiences is a gift. Each of those hard times made me stronger. It all led me to where I am today. I can do anything. I can be anything. And although I still struggle with the disease that we call depression, and the illness of anxiety, and PTSD, I am who I am for many reasons. I know what works for me and what doesn't. I had to learn to step aside when I'm anxious and take a moment just to breathe. I learned that exposure to things that once caused me extreme anxiety is a good thing. If ever I have an attack in public, whoever is with me knows to give me space to breathe (and keep other people away, even if they are wanting to help). I breathe it out, and eventually I am able to continue on with whatever I was doing. I am disabled mentally because of my disorders and illnesses (a left leg injury). But I get up each day and do my best to keep moving forward with life. I have my writing tools at home (for therapy and enjoyment), as well as: my books, my keyboard, running water, my back yard, walking trails, and the beach close by if ever I need to de-stress.

Be strong. These two words are far more powerful than I could've ever imagined. Throughout my life I repeated them over and over, until I was strong enough to keep moving forward.

I am surrounded by love, which is very important to keep me going. Life for me is good for right now. I say "right now" because I'm always aware that my illness can take change at any time. We cannot predict our future, but we can learn from our past. My illnesses do not define who I am, and they will not dictate who I am in the future.

It is important for all of us to take care of ourselves first, and not feel selfish about it. Life is truly a gift that we should handle with care.

If you or someone you know is struggling, please take the time to do whatever you can to help them. Kindness is a way of living, not a simple deed. Love changes everything.

CHAPTER TWO

Mindset, Mindfulness, and Mental Health

*"How I changed my life
by changing my thoughts."*

NICOLE THOMAS, CHRP, RYT 500

NICOLE THOMAS

As a yoga educator, Nicole works to infuse the practice of yoga into her students' daily lives to promote both physical and mental healing. Her classes focus on gentle and restorative yoga practices that bring calmness, clarity, and mindfulness to the yoga mat. It is her belief that yoga is truly for everyone regardless of age, gender, physical ability, or fitness level. In addition to Nicole's yoga training, she has a background in human resources and adult education. When not on her yoga mat, Nicole is a knitwear designer and pattern editor who always has a knitting project, or two, on the go. She enjoys combining her creativity, energy, mindfulness practices, and to share her love of knitting with others.

Nicole has an honors bachelor of arts degree from the University of Guelph in sociology, a post-graduate diploma from Durham College in human resources management, as well as a certificate in teaching and training adults. She's a member of the Human Resources Professional Association as a Certified Human Resources Professional (CHRP). She has completed a 500-hour yoga teacher training program and is registered with Yoga Alliance International (RYT 500).

www.nicolethomas.ca
ig: @nicolethomasryt | fb: @nicolethomasryt
li: @nicole-thomas-chrp

In hindsight, I have suffered from anxiety all my life. It was anxiety when I felt sick to my stomach every morning in grade three and always wanted to stay home from school. It was anxiety when I would obsess over deep philosophical questions like *why are we even here?* It was anxiety when, in my first year of university, I struggled to get up out of bed and go to class. It was anxiety when I lived in a foreign country, and struggled to leave my apartment and make friends. It was, and still is, anxiety when I sign up for something—a class, a workshop, or an event—and then don't end up going. I get these grand ideas of things I want to do and experience, but when the time comes to do and experience, I just can't.

Anxiety has always reared its ugly head. When it's mild, it shows up primarily as fatigue or bodily discomfort, such as stomach aches or headaches; when it's bad, it's panic attacks and tears.

And it took me nearly thirty-five years to realize what it was: anxiety.

My life has been pretty normal, and I have been extremely lucky. I did all the things I was "supposed to do." I got good grades in high school, then I went to university and got an honors degree. I have had the privilege to travel and even lived abroad for a while. I got a good job with good pay, benefits, and a pension. I was even so lucky as to meet a great guy, buy a house, and get engaged.

And then I got an even better paying job at the same organization. The job that, on paper, was my dream job.

But I was still not happy.

Sure, at home, I was doing okay. I had things I loved in my life: my amazing partner, our two adorable cats, more opportunities to travel the world, and hobbies that I loved. But I struggled to get up in the morning. I dreaded leaving the house. I cried in the bathroom at work. I took more sick days than I was proud of, and felt extreme amounts of guilt for doing so. I felt stuck. Lost. Confused. Over-whelmed. Bored.

I was awful to be around; my relationships were a mess and I hated everything about myself. I was impatient and hurtful with those who loved me.

When the panic attacks started, and I couldn't get through a day without one, a good friend suggested that I take some time off. I was fortunate enough to work for an organization that provided paid short-term disability leave for illness. I spent three weeks at home, to regroup. I was placed on an antidepressant to manage the anxiety, and given a tranquilizer for the panic attacks. But as soon as I left my work environment, I didn't really need them anymore. Other than the guilt of not being at work, suddenly I felt fine.

After a few weeks, I went back to work and things were better for a while.

Until they weren't.

Because I was still me.

This was the nature of my life. I'd make a change or start some-thing new. I'd feel content for a while, even happy. But then the boredom, worry, stress, laziness, fatigue would kick in, and I'd be back to where I started. Because even though I was changing my external world, I was still me on the inside.

As the saying goes, *wherever you go, there you'll be.*

I was making changes in my external life, but I wasn't doing the internal work. I was falling for the false belief that the exter-nal world should be the source of my happiness. That the material things, money, and achievements should be enough to bring me joy.

But I have learned that there is so much more than the world around us. What truly matters is our mindset. How we show up, think, and feel each day on the inside is what creates the world outside of us.

In the months after the major panic attacks had started and the sick leave had ended, I decided I had to do something different. I couldn't spend the next five years of my life, let alone thirty, in this cycle. I began to take action to learn, grow, and change.

I enrolled in a yoga teacher training program at my local yoga studio. I had practiced yoga on and off for many years, and the idea of becoming a yoga teacher always intrigued me. Perhaps it was my intuition guiding me. I was not an "advanced" yogi by any means, but I decided I would finally do it, even if it just meant learning how to do my downward-facing dog pose correctly.

And while I did learn proper alignment and structure for many poses, I learned so much more about myself. This learning has become invaluable in my healing journey.

Through the teachings of yoga, I have learned how my mindset and my subconscious mind directly impact my outlook on life. I changed my life by changing my thoughts.

> *"You need to learn how to select your thoughts just the same way you select your clothes every day. This is a power you can cultivate. If you want to control things in your life so bad, work on the mind. That's the only thing you should be trying to control."* -Elizabeth Gilbert

This concept was one of the pivotal "ah-ha" moments that has really transformed my life. The notion that we have control over our thoughts seemed so foreign to me at first. My thoughts just seemed like something that was happening to me, not a result of me. For most of us, our subconscious mind controls a lot of how we view ourselves and the world around us. And the sad thing is, our subconscious thought patterns are developed primarily when we are young children, before we have critical thinking skills, self-awareness, or any life experiences to support or verify those thoughts. What we are told, who other people think we are, and what experiences we have at this early age greatly influence how we think about ourselves and the world around us as adults. These stories continue to perpetuate themselves throughout our development years and into adulthood, and our subconscious mind continually looks for proof of these thoughts and stories in the world around us.[1]

Taking time off work for my anxiety and depression felt like the worst thing I could be doing, and the extreme guilt that came

---

1   Sincero, Jen. 2013. *You Are a Badass: How to Stop Doubting Your Greatness and Start Living an Awesome Life.* New York: Running Press Publishers.

along with it just heightened my anxious state. In my mind, it felt like the ultimate failure.

Who did I think I was? Only people who are lazy and entitled took stress or sick leave; who did I think I was to do something like that? I should be thankful just to have a job to go to each day. No one wants to go to work in the morning, but we just go and get it over with.

These and countless other thoughts created a feeling of guilt and shame around being mentally ill. Mainstream society and the media were all talking about mental health more and more, but I didn't think it really applied to me. In my head, I believed people would think I was taking advantage of the system for "just feeling sad."

But where did these thoughts come from?

Our point of view, perspective, mindset, beliefs all come from the society and culture we grow up in and the experiences of our parents and families before us. We are born into a system of rules, based in religion, law, even the primary language we speak, or the color of our skin. We don't choose where we enter this world, and these beliefs become a part of our reality before we take our first breath. As we grow and learn we see what is considered good being rewarded, and what is considered bad being punished, and we try our best to navigate our way through and follow these rules to the best of our ability. All because this is what we are supposed to do.[2]

The reality is that all the stories in our heads of who we are supposed to be, what we are supposed to be doing, and what path we are supposed to be following are not true. In my opinion, this is why there are so many of us suffering, managing, and living with anxiety.

> *"If we don't like the dream of our life, we need to change the agreements."*
> -don Miguel Ruiz

But we can change our reality. We can change those beliefs that were given to us and create new ones for ourselves. We can create a new story about what our life should look like and how we want to live it. We can find gratitude and appreciation for those who came

---

2   Ruiz, don Miguel.. 1997. *The Four Agreements: A Practical Guide to Personal Freedom (A Toltec Wisdom Book).* Carlsbad: Hay House, Inc.

before us, and we can recognize that what works for everyone else may not work for you or for me—and that is okay.

When the damaging thoughts, self-doubt, negative feelings, worry, or fear—however anxiety decides to show up that day—begin, I ask myself one question: *is it true?* Is it true for me, in this moment, in this decision, in this lifetime? Nine times out of ten, the answer is no.

Then I change the story.

If someone said to me now, "You should just be grateful to have a job," something I have heard a lot in the past when I said I was unhappy in my career—instead of thinking they are right and feeling guilty for being ungrateful, and for all the people who are living in poverty and unemployment, which is where my anxious brain would always go—I now can ask myself, "Is that true?" Should I truly be grateful to just be employed? Is that truly the sum of my existence? Of course not. Yes, I need money to contribute to my household bills and responsibilities. But my job does not define who I am and is not the source of my happiness.

We are here to live our best life and find joy in doing. For me, that meant leaving a corporate job with a long commute that did not feed my soul, despite the fact that it paid really well. I didn't want to wait thirty years to retire and then begin to live my best life. I wanted to do it now.

Today, I am mindful of the thoughts that enter my brain and the negative impact they can have on my anxious mind if I don't control and change them.

And if my anxious mind does take over, I forgive myself. I am kind to myself. I know I am allowed to have moments of sadness, grief, stress, anxiety—I have given myself permission. Beating ourselves up for feeling this way just makes us feel worse. I accept that anxiety is part of my life, I allow it to just be what it is, and then I let it go. I take a nap if I need to. I cry if I need to. Then I move on and try again.

Being mindful of my thoughts and emotions has also helped me to live more in the present, and spend less time worrying about the past or stressing about the future. When I live in the present moment, choose positive thoughts and perspectives, and truly experience the joy of living life, I am less anxious. By being in the here and now, being grateful for where I am and what I am experiencing, I am able to reduce my anxiety over what I think I should be doing because in that moment, it doesn't matter.

Practicing gratitude also helps me to choose positive thoughts. Being grateful for what you have in your life—in a single moment, a day, a week, or even a year—can shift your perspective and mindset. Instead of getting irritated or stressed about what I may have given up in terms of my career and finances, I am grateful that I don't have to commute long hours or sit behind a desk all day. I am grateful that I get to spend more time with my cats, more time on my knitwear designs and creative outlets, and more time teaching others how they can feel better in their minds and bodies through yoga. A gratitude practice doesn't have to be complicated. It can be just noticing in a single moment what you can be grateful for: the sunrise, a good cup of coffee, an afternoon nap. Or it can be more in-depth through journalling or meditation. It will be different for everyone. For example, I have tried keeping a gratitude journal, but I've discovered that finding gratitude moment by moment feels much easier and more grounding.

Living with anxiety can still be strenuous. While these practices have helped reduce my feelings of anxiety day-to-day, they still pop in to say "hello" on a regular basis. But, thanks to the lessons I have learned through the practice of yoga, mindfulness, and gratitude, I am better equipped to deal with my anxiety. Not only has being mindful of my thoughts and mindset helped me to change my approach to life each day, it has also given me the strength to let go when the change doesn't come so easily. I am more confident in my decisions and the life I have chosen to lead. I have the opportunity to share what I love—the teachings of yoga with my students—and to embrace the new thoughts and experiences I am creating with open arms.

And despite it being a challenging journey, I am grateful for my experience. I truly believe that things in life happen for a reason and that the universe is looking out for us all. I believe that these experiences were meant to happen to me; struggling, managing, and living with anxiety is part of who I am, and is helping me to create a more meaningful life.

A life that is more than just about existing.

CHAPTER THREE

Can I Get Some Boundaries Please?

"You have the inalienable right to set boundaries and protect your mental well-being."

NICOLE TAYLOR EBY

Nicole Taylor Eby is a budding new author, a mother of three, and a military career woman. Currently residing in Victoria, British Columbia, Nicole has a love of the outdoors and is working on mastering the art of sailing. She is raising twins while serving with the Royal Canadian Navy. She is working to keep a balance between working and mothering while finding her escape through the written word—including an upcoming series of romance novels.

With over twenty years of learning about resilience, self-motivation, and finding joy in life, Nicole brings to the table a refreshing take on life, love, and the ups and downs of thriving in today's hectic world.

Nicole developed a chronic illness due to emotional trauma, and is now on a path to create tranquility and calm in her life through setting clear and strong boundaries and by sharing her story so that others might learn from it.

nicoletayloreby.com
ig: @nicole_taylor_eby_author | fb: @nicoletayloreby

"It's okay. It's okay. It's okay," I repeated over and over, sitting in my driveway as I gathered the courage to go inside. I spoke so quickly that my words sounded more like hyperventilation than a soothing mantra. My breathing was fast and shallow, making me lightheaded, as I fought to calm the panic. I fumbled for the pills in my purse. The pills that my doctor had prescribed to me so that I could enter my own home.

I ran through my list of "Should I's?" and their respective buts. *Should I speak up? But she is his mom, and she is dying . . . Should I confront her? But I always end up looking like an uncompassionate, self-centred bitch . . . Should I insist she leave my home? But what kind of person kicks out a terminally ill family member?*

When my mother-in-law became terminally ill with cancer and the treatment was not available where she lived, I invited her into my home. This decision would be both my emotional downfall and the start of my healing journey.

At first, things seemed fine. She was emotional and difficult to talk to, but I chalked it up to a natural reaction to receiving a diagnosis that was a death sentence.

Things unraveled very quickly.

Little by little, I started to feel undermined by her actions. She would do things to exclude me or make me look bad to my husband and friends, and she would make comments that hinted at my not having a place in the family.

Her actions were subtle. I felt like I was going crazy. I knew something was not right, but I did not know what to do.

I did not know how to set boundaries, so I let the emotional abuse continue. It was not until I needed to take medication to go into my own home that I tried to stand up for myself. Except my actions were not standing up for myself. What I did was offer to go and stay with my mom so that I would not be making things more difficult for anyone.

That is right: I offered to leave my own home so that my mother-in-law would be comfortable. And yet I was accused of being unwelcoming and unhelpful.

My emotional pain had become so extreme that I saw no alternative other than to run away. I spent every day tip-toeing around, trying not to break the eggshells I was walking on, and having no success because they were not really eggshells, but cleverly laid, emotionally-destructive traps.

> *"Loneliness and feeling unwanted is the most*
> *terrible kind of poverty."* -Mother Theresa

The isolation was so acute that I started to believe I was truly not worthy of being loved because if I was worth loving, then why was nobody willing to hear my story?

Alone in my room, I cried soul-shattering sobs of grief.

My husband tried to be supportive, but he was trapped between his mother and his wife, and she was clever enough to keep her actions hidden from him. I was trying to protect him from having to choose between us. It was difficult for him to see that the situation went beyond personality conflict.

I tried reaching out to friends, but they did not step up to support me. In fact, quite the opposite happened. They did not believe me. They judged me, thinking that I had no compassion for this woman who was dying in my home.

This response from my support network was devastating. I desperately needed someone to just be on my side.

I wanted to say, "Stop," but it felt like there was nobody there to stand behind me, and I was not strong enough to say it alone.

For years, even after she died, I struggled with anger toward a person who would never apologize. It did not matter that she could no longer hurt me. What mattered was that I had let her destroy my life, and I was angry.

I was not able to begin healing until I realized that I needed to tell my story. I needed to be heard, and I needed to learn how to set boundaries.

My mother-in-law would never have been able to emotionally abuse me, and I would have been able to stand up for myself, if I had believed that I was in a position to say, "No." At the core of that ability are boundaries.

I chose to stay quiet despite having severe panic attacks because I had been taught that I must never disappoint. I must do whatever is necessary to make sure everyone around me is happy; this meant being a gracious hostess no matter the behavior of the guest. It meant that I should always open my home to family members in distress, even if they were violating my personal rights and attacking my emotional health.

It took me a long time to find my voice. It took a life-changing chronic condition for me to tell my story and start taking back my power. The power that I had slowly given away each time I did not stand up for myself. Each time a man touched me inappropriately, and I said nothing; each time that I was marginalized in my job because I was a woman in a male-dominated field, and I just smiled and worked harder; and each time that someone took advantage of me, and I allowed it because "good girls" don't make a fuss.

Each time that I did not set a clear boundary.

I believe that a boundary is a line you draw that you do not let anyone cross for any reason. It is saying, "No" to the wants or actions of others that harm you or do not align with your values. It is standing up for yourself. It is where your beliefs meet the beliefs of other people and society. It can be as simple as saying, "I do not want sandwiches for lunch" or as complicated as refusing to allow a family member into your home because they do not treat you with respect.

So, what can you do? How can you learn to set boundaries?

It is not something you are going to master overnight. Quite honestly, I am still struggling to stand true to my boundaries. It is something that requires practice. I also cannot set your boundaries for you. Boundaries are personal. What I can do is give you the tools that I have used to start establishing my own boundaries.

What is important to remember is that whenever the question starts with "should," then we are exploring boundaries. And those "shoulds" are often followed by excuses and harsh self-judgements.

When we are born, society assigns us roles. If you are born a girl, then there are certain expectations placed on you the moment you emerge: nurturer, mother, good girl, to name a few. While embracing these roles is positive and soul-nourishing for some, these roles also do have significant power to harm because at their heart is the idea that a woman's self-worth is tied to what others think of her.

And if you are going to challenge those roles, then you are going to disappoint someone.

> *"Care about what other people think, and you*
> *will always be their prisoner."*
> -Lao Tzu

As a young girl, I quickly learned that I was expected to be a people-pleaser, and by the time I was a young adult, my entire self-worth was inextricably linked to what others thought of me. I was frightened to put one foot out of place. At the root of my fear was my inability to set boundaries—because a "good girl" does not say "No." I became terrified of conflict because if there was conflict, it meant that I had done something wrong.

You cannot set boundaries without some level of conflict.

My life has been marked by my belief that what people think of me is more important than my own personal well-being: aka, my lack of boundaries. The fallout from my lack of boundaries was traumatic. As a teenager, I developed an eating disorder and struggled with suicidal ideation; as a young adult, I struggled with crippling depression and anxiety; as an adult, I stayed in unhealthy relationships because I was desperately seeking approval; and now, as I enter middle age, I have been consumed by crippling, full-body chronic pain. Chronic pain that has its roots in emotional rather than physical trauma, because emotional pain that is suppressed can result in physical illness.

Boundaries are essential to emotional well-being because without boundaries, we leave ourselves vulnerable to the actions of others. Everyone has the right to set both physical and mental boundaries. In the United Nations Universal Declaration of Human Rights, we are afforded the right to life, which can be defined as having the right to live in freedom and safety.[1] This right includes psychological safety. No one has the right to treat you in a way that harms your emotional well-being. It does not matter what their circumstances are. It does not matter if they are dying.

> *"Daring to set boundaries is about having the courage to love ourselves even when we risk disappointing others."* -Brené Brown

HOW TO SET BOUNDARIES

1. Get to know yourself.

The first step in setting boundaries involves looking inward. What do you believe in? What is important to you? What is okay and not okay to happen to you? Different people will have different answers.

A difficult part of this process is exploring your dark areas. We all have scars from the traumas that life has dealt us, and we have to understand them to really know ourselves.

It is important to remember that trauma does not have to be big to be damaging. Little traumas can build up and impact your concept of self-worth—and thus your ability to set boundaries.

2. Discover your self-worth.

A large piece of being able to set boundaries is the belief that you are worthy of those boundaries. If you do not believe that you have the right to say "No," then even if you do know where your line in the sand should be, you will not be able to defend it. Everyone is worthy and has the right to determine where their limits are. Everyone has the right to decide what is okay and not okay.

When it comes to our emotional rights, one person is not more important than another. We are not rank-ordered, with the person at the top getting to choose which rights they want to honor and the person at the bottom getting whatever crumbs are left. The CEO is

---

1   Youth For Human Rights. (n.d.) "What Are Human Rights?" Accessed July 30, 2019. https://www.youthforhumanrights.org/what-are-human-rights/universal-declaration-of-human-rights/articles-1-15.html

not more important than the janitor. The Prime Minister is not more important than the voter. My mother-in-law was not more important than me.

It does not matter what your story is, and it doesn't matter what their story is—boundaries are boundaries, and you have the right to set them.

3. Practice setting small boundaries.

When you are making a change, it is always good to start small. Just like with any new skill, it is going to take some practice to get effective and confident at setting boundaries. Intentionally setting smaller, less significant boundaries, such as requiring that everyone remove their shoes when they come into your home, provides a strong foundation for tackling the major boundaries, such as insisting that a person living in your home treats you with respect.

4. Keep yourself accountable: journal.

Learning to set boundaries involves changing habits, and it is easy to slip back into our old way of doing things. One way to ensure that enforcing your boundaries becomes a habit is to keep yourself accountable by tracking your progress.

Using a journal is one powerful way to track your progress. It doesn't need to be anything fancy, and you do not need to be a writer to use one. Just jot down the times when you did or did not stand up for yourself so you can look for patterns in your behavior. These patterns can help to identify the triggers that are undermining your determination to enforce your boundaries.

5. Seek help from others.

Finally, I encourage you to seek help from others. You do not have to do this alone; in fact, you might even progress more quickly if you have someone watching your back.

There are two types of help that are critical to the process. The first is professional counselling or therapy. The second is finding a loved one to be a boundary-holder for you.

A boundary-holder is someone who helps you ensure that your boundaries are honored. They point out to you and others when your boundaries are being violated. It takes strength to stand firm, strength that you might not have at first. While you are learning, it can work wonders to have someone help you hold the line until you are able to do it for yourself.

There is no shame in needing help. It is the entire reason humans crave connection and community: we cannot do this alone and were never meant to.

The price of silence is much greater than the price of speaking up.

It is *never* too late to draw a line in the sand, to claim your boundary. It does not matter how many times you have kept silent before or said, "Yes" when you meant "No." You can choose to say, "No" at any moment. My moment came when I could not physically hold it in any longer. My psychological rights had been breached, and it did not matter what trump card she had; I was within my rights to say, "enough."

Even as I write now, there is a part of me that is afraid. There is a part of me that wants to tell a different story because my family, friends, and co-workers are going to know my truth. It won't be my dirty little secret, festering in my soul, any longer. It will be out there in broad daylight. And my revelation might hurt some of them.

A part of me still wants to make excuses for her; she was, after all, dying. But here is what I know to be true: she violated my personal bill of rights, and there is *no* excuse for that. I may not be able to have justice, but I can begin to heal by telling my story, both so that I am heard and so that someone else might recognize herself in my truth.

I am pleased to be able to say that I am coming through, and I am stronger. I have recognized that while it was her responsibility to respect my psychological rights, it was *my job* to set clear boundaries and insist they be honored. Knowledge is power, and power is strength. I can let the hurt go because I have the power to make it happen, and the strength to begin a new chapter in which I stand up for my rights as a woman and as a human being.

And perhaps I owe her a degree of thanks, because I learned a powerful lesson. I learned that I am important. I learned that it's okay to set boundaries—in fact, it is my right as a human being. So I am stronger for the experience.

It is my fervent hope that through reading my story, another woman will see her own worth and recognize that she, too, has the right to set boundaries.

CHAPTER FOUR

; and Then . . .

"To the girl I was before: I love you and forgive you."

CASSAUNDRA NOYES

CASSAUNDRA NOYES

Cassaundra Noyes spends her time teaching middle school social studies, and by night she follows her passion as a photographer and videographer. She spends most of her time adventuring in the woods with her dog, Indie, in Northern Alberta. She is grateful for the friends who have become family and her weekly phone calls with her Nan. Never short on adventure, she is determined to travel the world. This chapter is her letting go. A bucket list item, a check mark to say that she would not be defined by the mistakes of the past. She thanks you for being a part of her healing. May this book inspire you to share your own story, and remind you that you are not alone. You are now a piece in her story. We walk together.

birchandbonecreative@gmail.com
ig: @birchandbonecreative

I caught the reflection, the dark glass illuminated by a broken, sunken face. My face, one I couldn't recognize, one I didn't want to acknowledge. I was embarrassed, lying in a hospital gown on an uncomfortable bed on the psychiatric floor. No sharp objects and no way to contact the outside world. I felt more alone than ever and unprepared to face the reality; which was that I felt I had failed.

Six hours earlier, I had written my goodbye letters, sent emails, locked my dog in my room after saying goodbye, and lined the pill bottles along the counter of my bathroom sink. The person I stared at then was a different person than I see now. Determined, she held a sense of peace that was terrifying and relatable. She had given up and the exhaustion of trying to trudge through another day had fled. She was me, and I didn't have to anymore. Suicide would be the solution to my heart break, loneliness, and emptiness. No one would miss me. I left no one to care; everyone moved on after death, and so everything would be taken care of.

If you find something relatable in these words, I want you to read the next bit carefully. My battle with suicide was induced by what the psychologist called reactive depression. It wasn't that I was too sad, selfish, or broken. This type of depression can be brought on by any trauma or intense situation in your life. Everyone with reactive depression is different, and what triggers me may not trigger you. A person experiencing reactive depression is a person going through trauma. My trauma was grief.

I believe we often overlook the losses we have in our lives. We associate grief with the death of a loved one or pet. Loss came to me in other ways as well. It came in the loss of a job, my mom, my partner, his family, my everyday normal, and the dreams I had built and counted on. I want to remind you: our traumas and our hurt, they can't be measured against someone else's. Our mental strength is not determined by what we can handle, but more so by what we will preserve and work through. Growing up, I had a lot of exposure to grief: I had lost family members and homes. My dad had walked out of our life because of alcohol abuse when I was a teenager. There was a lot of loss. But nothing could have prepared me for the insurmountable loss I was about to face as I turned twenty-five.

To set the scene: I was living in Australia with my long-term partner. We had scored our dream jobs, had a cute little cottage in a small town, and had adopted a lab puppy named Indie. At this stage in life, I had a strained relationship with my mom. I don't think she or any of my family understood my blind faith in following my heart or my need to wander this Earth. She was an amazing mom in her own way, but I think somewhere she was dealing with a lot of her own trauma. She struggled to show love in traditional ways and, true to form, had her own quirky way of doing things.

My partners' parents, on the other hand, were great. They were kind, welcoming, and fearlessly showed their love for their children much differently than I had known in my own life. We were close to his family, as mine pushed away.

Like all my friends, I was on Pinterest creating boards of home design, engagement rings, and my future wedding. My partner and I portrayed a life that was on track to happily ever after. Sometimes though, for whatever reason, the fairy tale is not always the plan. In this story, Cinderella didn't get Prince Charming and someone died. While living in Australia my partner became unhappy and irrationally moved us back to his parents. We paused and started conversations around plans to build a life we both wanted. Then came the news that my mom was sick. It was the week before Easter, and I remember getting a message: they had found a lump. It was the first time I had talked to my mom in months. I missed her. She tried her best, but I could hear the fear in her voice as she told me the story of a developing cold, which turned to pneumonia that she was too stubborn to go get checked out. In a conversation, before the night she passed, she admitted to knowing that something was seriously wrong with her health, but not wanting to face it. I think we often do the same with our mental health. How often do we know we're sad, angry, numb, distracted, etc., but it's not something physical we can get "checked"? I hope that this book serves as a push for more of us to treat our sadness like a cold, and for those we turn to professionally to treat it with as much attention as our bodies receive, and with the love our souls deserve.

Waiting for the results of my mom's biopsy felt like forever. Being in Australia had always made me feel far away, but this made me feel farther. Her diagnosis was unknown for a week, and I will never forget the call that finally came: stage four lung cancer.

As my partner and I began making plans to head back to Canada, he suddenly broke off our relationship. He was in love with someone else he had met online in Australia. Someone I didn't know existed, someone who had taken my place. I packed a suitcase and said goodbye to the family I so desperately wanted to be a part of. I left the life I had built only to return home and say goodbye to the life I had run away from.

When I arrived in Canada I felt like I was at the front line of a war zone. I spent two weeks caring for my mom, not being allowed to talk about death, or what I was going through. I was instructed by family members to put on a happy face and save my breakdowns for when I was alone. It was mornings of taking panicked ambulance rides, contacting family, trying to figure out what she needed, and watching her struggle to breathe. It was hell for everyone, especially her.

The night before her death, I got to have a real honest conversation with my mom. We talked about life and all of the things she wanted to do. She asked me the hardest question I've ever been asked: "Am I dying?"

The weeks that followed were a blur of protocol, ceremony, hoop-jumping, and casserole-receiving. She was gone, he was gone, my family was gone, and everyone was trying to survive on their own instead of coming together. I was an "adult" but I did not understand what I was doing and nothing in my schooling, university, life had prepared me to deal with the "what next."

I returned to Australia to start over again, mainly because I didn't know what else to do. The thought of staying in my hometown where my mom had died was overwhelming. I didn't know how to deal with the grief and loss I was feeling. As much as my life started to look like it was being put back together, there were so many unanswered questions that weighed on me. I did my best, but we are not superheroes. I think we are capable of great things, but we all have limits and I found mine.

* * *

When they released me from the hospital, I had to cut the bullshit. As much as I wanted to be, I wasn't invincible, or immune to how hard life had become. I realized that my struggle with mental health was just beginning. My one-off therapy session and handful of Valium wasn't my cure, and realistically I would struggle with my reactionary depression for the rest of my life. I had been trying to fix everything, rebuild everything, and be everything I needed on my own. My psychology girl crush, Jody Carrington, author of *Kids These Days*, often says that "kids are not attention-seeking, they are connection-seeking." —So are adults. After everything I went through, I had to face the embarrassment of continuing on, the judgement of "she only did it to get attention" or "she will do anything to get him back." I was so deeply craving connection with the world because everything I had known had ceased to be there. Reflecting back now, I see that I had to learn two lessons: how to make new connections and how to love the battle.

So now what?

Six years later, I can tell you that I'm still working on these things. While I wouldn't change anything I went through, I still struggle sometimes with waking up in the morning. Making friends isn't easy, and letting people in is even harder. So what do we do when nothing goes as planned and we're sad sometimes?

For me it was therapy. Therapy is a necessary evil. I was reluctant, hesitant, and downright "tantrum-y" about going to therapy. I didn't see the value in revisiting the same events repeatedly. I was sick of my story. What I learned, though, is that the more I told it, the more I worked through it, the less of a victim I became. It started to be a point of empowerment and a platform from which to make change. I also want you to know that I didn't see just one therapist or have just one session. I saw many therapists over the course of years with no certain time frame.

I also ran into a lot of barriers and had to learn how to accept help. For example, I had no money. A two-hundred-dollar session was a splurge, that didn't seem worth it while I was in survival mode.

AND THEN . . .

Friends and those I love helped me out. They paid for services, used connections through their church, and downright pushed me to do it. I will forever be grateful. When you're in a dark time, it's hard to accept help. If you're like me, you will struggle with feelings of unworthiness and disconnection. *Why would someone want to help me?* This is why making connections is so important. If you know someone feeling like this, please be gentle. It has nothing to do with you; it's them trying to become vulnerable. That skill has taken me a solid six years to gain, and I'm still working on it. I'm grateful to those who didn't give up on me.

The healing process taught me there are a lot of different therapies out there. For the longest time, I hated talking. It made me feel uncomfortable.The stigma of suicide is that it's selfish, and sometimes I felt like I was trying to convince this stranger I wasn't crazy. I think my view on therapy switched after I attended a few sessions with a sandbox therapist. This was by far my favorite type, and I encourage everyone to seek this therapy at least once in your life. The therapist's room was set up like a giant toy sandbox. On one wall there was nothing but plastic figurines. In my session, after the therapist asked her question, I had a very limited time to answer her by creating a scene in the sand with whatever figurines spoke to me. Then she analyzed and helped me work through it. It was incredible.

There are so many ways you can reach out for help nowadays. Online sessions, Instagram accounts like Bell Let's Talk, your religious leaders, community, etc. As we get less afraid to acknowledge that we are not immune to the hardships of life, there will rise a higher demand for each person to be taught skills that perhaps our parents could never teach us, life couldn't teach us. Don't be afraid to train your brain, heart, and soul. Our mental and spiritual health needs that training for when things get hard.

This amazing book is all about no longer being silent, so let me leave you with the last truth I've learned on this journey: suicide, in whatever stage, is not selfish. I was sad, lonely, overwhelmed, and depressed, and wanted so badly to have just one moment in which I didn't have to feel these things. As a teacher, I see a handful of young adolescents each year who struggle with how hard life is. These young students are not selfish. Their hard is their hard, and not for us to judge. They are lonely and afraid. They are craving connection and love. So often we hear, "People who attempt suicide are so selfish." When we are looking for a life-line, these words echo in our society and disconnect us even more.

Suicidal attempts happen in my field of work more than I'd like to admit. It's part of our collective mental health story in this modern society, and I've had people from all walks of life admit to feeling this way at some point. My journey has allowed me to use my story to connect with little ones, friends, and strangers, who feel the same. The best thing we can do is always show love. If you relate to this story, please know you are not selfish, you are just struggling. I was not selfish. That's a fact I've worked hard to acknowledge and own. I am just a girl who lost her mom. In that, I lost my way . . . for a little bit.

CHAPTER FIVE

The Best Gift Ever: Discovering Your Value

"You may think the rest of the world has something to share but never underestimate what you can bring to the world."

VIOLAINE PIGEON

VIOLAINE PIGEON

Following her studies at the University of Montreal as a dietician, Violaine Pigeon started a clinician career in the largest hospital in Quebec. She learned there how to create a positive influence on others, to help them reach their health goals, and to interact with her peers to become a real teammate in the wellbeing of their patients.

Her personal experiences led her to become a healthy living role model, a positive example, and a balanced person for her family first, and for the rest of the world. She always wants to reflect the things she teaches.

Over the years, Violaine became a motivating nutritionist and a wellness creator. She sees the good in every situation, and she transmits it to her clients. She believes that humans can reach all that they can dream. Recently, she became an invested fitness athlete, a mother of two magnificent happy small humans, and a wife-to-be.

Violaine lives close to Montreal, with her two kids, Olivier and Chloé, and her fiancé Vincent. She speaks French, but always reads in English. To have the opportunity to write in an English book was part of her bucket list, as this is a wonderful way to touch and reach people's soul, and give them wings.

ig: @Violaine.athlete | fb: @Violaine Pigeon
li: @Violaine Pigeon

When I was a kid, I had no doubt—I was convinced—I would achieve my goals, my dreams, my expectations. My family was one of those where there was no difference between a boy and a girl—I have a twin brother and we learned everything together, regardless of our gender. When we were young my father was very maternal, as was my mother.

During the teen part of my life, I started to struggle with my perception of myself. I compared every aspect of me to others, and disliked it. Doubt ran through me, in my head, in my confidence, in my beliefs.

This began when I used to dance as a ballerina. The teachers compared all students, their physiques, their strengths, and their aptitudes. I was not as good as I wanted to be; I was too tall, my legs were too long, my breasts too big, to be a classic dancer. Because of this new vision of myself, I had developed eating disorders, social dependences, and an absolute low self-esteem. I met bad guys and had relationships with them just to try to find love for myself through their eyes. I was of course totally wrong, but I was stuck in a complex wheel I could not stop.

When it came time to go to college, I decided to go to a school far from my hometown. I felt it was an option to break with this past, and to restart my life without others' pressure on me to be as they thought I was—fragile, shy, affection dependent, and kind of average. Honestly, it was a great move. I fought hard to stay true to my deep belief system, to allow myself to believe I can do everything as my family taught me. I also started to take my studies seriously and began to succeed in different classes. It was a good time in my life, but it did not last long.

At seventeen years old, my health decreased to the point I was admitted to the hospital because even though I was eating enough, I had lost a lot of weight and had terrible abdominal pain every hour of the day. After much time, I received a diagnosis: Crohn Disease;

an incurable chronic condition. For the rest of my life. At this age, it was particularly tough. They talked to me about surgeries to help me have a normal life, but nothing about a cure. I started many medications that made me gain weight, more than double what I weighed when I was hospitalized. It was another terrible moment for my confidence, I stopped believing in myself again, and I had to accept a body that was not mine.

Years passed; I learned how to manage my health and my medication and I graduated as a nutritionist with a university degree. I met a good man and we got married after two years together. We bought our dream house and we had our two lovely kids. I was happy, and back to feeling like myself for years. I wanted to be a role model for my growing kids.

* * *

I used to work for the same company for eight years when I got promoted for a national position. It was a huge success for me and my family. I had the opportunity to travel across Canada each month through this new position, and was absolutely satisfied professionally. My new boss was a woman from Halifax, so we had mostly virtual and phone relations; we met maybe three times in person. I felt stressed working with her; she was tough and harsh towards me. She gave me files to manage and cancelled them the day before my deadline—she cancelled many projects that I had worked very hard on, especially hard because I had to work in English (my second language, as I am a French-Canadian). After many months of this regimen of cancelling nearly all the projects I was involved in, it was time for our year-end evaluation. My boss and I met in Montreal for this, and it was a horrible experience. She talked to me about my maternity leaves, as if it was a mistake to take advantage of it twice. She criticized my language skills and my speed of work, as it was slower than my colleagues. She made rude comments throughout the discussion, spoke negatively about my province (Quebec), as we were the only part of the country to not understand the rest because of our language skills. It was an hour of totally disappointing comments about me, a few close colleagues, my political world (my province of the country), my work, and my capacities. After wasting many hours and energy on cancelled projects, I was tired, exhausted, annihilated. I lost myself in my work because I did it with all my integrity, my capacities, and my heart. I was then told I was not enough. In the meantime, I experienced a crisis in my marriage and we were about to divorce. It was too much. I was miserable. I felt like I was in the middle of a major breakdown.

My doctor tried a few medications to help me recover. It was not a real success. I still could not take care of myself. I feared going out of my house, afraid of people. I could not ask for help from family or friends, unable to admit I had been strong for too long that I had now become broken. I just felt weak, never enough, and lost in my own life. I felt terribly empty.

One day, I had a call from my insurance program. They had a suggestion to help me as all the medications I tried didn't make a difference after months of trying alongside therapies. They suggested starting physical activity to stimulate positive hormonal secretion in my brain. It was terrifying—I feared people and going out of my home, and they asked me to meet a personal coach in a gym.

So, I found a very cool gym coach. He met me alone, and suggested that he coach me in a complete empty gym for my first couple of sessions. This is how we started. After a couple of weeks, I was comfortable to be with another girl in the gym, and then, with two or three strangers. I started to enjoy those sessions and looked forward to it each week. The positive effect appeared; I felt a bit better in my body; I discovered some abilities I never thought I had; I was even stronger than expected, and it started to reflect in my mind. After a few months, I was in the gym four times a week, and once by myself. To make sure I wouldn't run into people who knew me, I drove forty-five minutes to a gym far from my hometown, I was more comfortable when I was alone, and believe me, it was the best way for me. As I was in the gym by myself, another coach noticed how serious I was about my workouts, and noticed my gains. He came to me and suggested we start a challenge: he offered me to try to reach a competition level of physical condition. This excited me! I was ready for something new, and I always enjoyed being challenged. I did not think about it for long before accepting his offer.

It took me six months of food management and specific training to be ready for the stage. In total, I spent more than a year becoming the new me. I did my first fitness competition as a bikini athlete in April 2013. To my surprise I received third place! What a win for me after all this! This meant more than a fitness placement for me, it meant I was able to feel great and succeed again for the first time after losing every parcel of belief in myself. Surely, it was only the beginning.

I was thirty-five years old when I started my fitness journey, thirty-six when I got up on stage for the first time. As of today, in 2020, I stopped counting the number of stages I have been on after the fifteenth. My athlete sheet is kind of a dream, because I've placed in every single competition I went through. At forty-three years old, I know who I am because of this journey; and if you ask me if I would love to modify a part of my life, my answer will for sure be NO. If I did not go through all of this, I would never know me as I am today. I would never be at the place I have found.

Through this journey, I met new friends and our relationships are based on the real me. They are not all from within the fitness world, but they all respect my discipline and my choices because I enjoy it so much. I discovered how much I love being stronger by the time I practice my sport, and it is reflected in my mind and in my soul. I am more peaceful today than I ever was, I feel I am the best role model for my kids that I dreamed to be, and I teach them what I learned the hard way.

Today, I apply what I've learned in the fitness world in all the spheres of my life. When I feel like I am not strong enough or prepared enough for a project at work, for a negotiation, or for a complex problem to solve, I remember where I started—from the very bottom—and I am convinced I can reach excellence if I put in the work needed. I know I can do anything if I practice and strive to be better. I learned how to focus, and I know confidence can bring success. I love the picture I developed in my mind: life and its challenges are like a weight-bar in the gym. It can be hard to figure out how to lift it, but if I only focus on picking up the bar and visualize lifting it, believe it or not, in the end, I will. Every single time. Not always with the first attempt, but if I put the work in, eventually, I can lift it. It is never as hard as I first thought.

* * *

I learned to never listen to the dream stealers; to never pay attention to negative people who try to tell me I won't be able to do something; they will never take my power again. I will never keep my voice silent as I did before; I am valuable and enough, I will reach every goal that I desire. I stopped accepting fake and toxic people around me, because I am worth more and choose who and what comes into my world; it is a reflection on me. I am not afraid anymore to tell someone my limits and when I have reached them. I learned to love myself as I am, and I take time to tell myself positive things each day. I am not perfect, this is not what I am saying; I am who I am, and I am working to the best possible version of me. I do everything to be a good human being and to act as a role model for people. I sleep well thinking of who I am because each thing I do is relevant to my deep values. I now know that every human-being is a valuable resource, they are the most valuable asset to the world. They are all needed, so I know I have my place here and I am not afraid to say it anymore.

Know that being unsatisfied or having poor self-esteem is not the only way of existing. I learned this my own way, and I sincerely wish for you to discover this more easily than I did. If I can give some quick advice, it would be to stop looking for what you want outside, look for what you want to BE inside. You will discover more than you think—you are beautiful, unique, true, valuable, enough, and strong. You will find things you want to develop more, and you will attract people who can help you, positively. You need to accept it without being shy of who you are. Don't be afraid to shine, you deserve the light you give off. You may not know it, but you are for sure a model for somebody else. Because of who you are, what you think, and how you act. You are better than you think, and you have to recognise it. You may never know who is watching, but you are the star for somebody else. Start to see yourself this way and you will discover so many other good points in you. The most difficult is to start, and just because you read this, you are about to do it; do not hesitate to write your own characteristics down. You could come back to it someday when you feel uncertain, and remember you ARE how you describe your positive self, however you may feel, this could bring you back to yourself.

Imagine everything about yourself with good words.

Imagine everyone brings good to others.

Imagine everyone believes in themself and stops being afraid of what they can achieve.

Imagine learning from others who are better at something instead of being jealous or afraid of them.

It took me a while to learn and to be who I am today, but I have no regrets. Many people never discover themselves. I wish you to show the world who you are and what you are capable of. I wish you to find yourself and to love you, as beautiful and strong as you are. Do not waste your time overthinking it, and just start doing it. Over analysis is paralysis—I went through it for years. Skip this part and start living, start saying and start enjoying. Every minute counts. Love is life, so start with you and the rest will follow.

SECTION TWO

Each Time a Woman Stands for Herself She Stands for All Women

There is an undeniable truth that victims of abuse and domestic violence share: although you may come out victorious, you will not come out unscathed. Abuse changes you.

FEATURING

Lori Williamson
Charleyne Oulton
Courtney Battie
Lindsay Whitham
Mlle Elizabeth Ann
Sasha Rose
Amber Phillips

"I survived because the fire
inside me burned stronger
than the fire around me"

-RUMI

CHAPTER SIX

Just Get Over It!

"Health is the greatest of wealth and a positive mindset is the most powerful currency."

LORI WILLIAMSON

LORI WILLIAMSON

Lori Williamson is a mother of two amazing humans, a retired registered nurse, pastoral care provider, missionary, and a grief recovery specialist. She is a student of life, writer, and an animal lover. Being a health enthusiast, Lori is also a yoga and paddle board instructor. Traumas made an unwelcome entrance into her life at the age of four starting a battle with PTSD, anxiety, and depression. She openly shares her story hoping to raise awareness and empower others. Pen-to-paper to release the pain was her therapy.

Her life experiences lead to her mission of bringing attention to social injustices, particularly child sex slavery and human trafficking. Lori is a supporter of two much-needed organizations and is committed to help children heal from trauma. The first, Mighty Oaks Global Initiatives in Thailand works with children at risk and their families, to support and supplement educational costs for children through to university. The second, Destiny Rescue is an organization that is expanding worldwide to fight the growing sexual slavery demands. Each day rescue agents put their lives on the line searching and rescuing young, weak, defenceless, and forgotten children that are held captive, used, abused, tortured, and forced to live in inhumane conditions. The children are then rescued and educated. Lori is committed to helping others transform their emotional pain into self compassion and their grief into gratitude. Lori's life experiences are her "why." No child should be violated especially by people holding power and trust.

www.transformestudio.com
ig: @Happypretzel44 | @Transformeyoga
fb: @Lori Williamson | li: @Lori Williamson | t: @Transformeyoga

"Most people are good and occasionally do something they know is bad. Some people are bad and struggle every day to keep it under control. Others are corrupt to the core and they don't give a damn, as long as they don't get caught. But evil is a completely different creature. Evil is bad that believes it is good." -Karen Marie Moning

"Just get over it!" My husband stood annoyed with his arms crossed over his chest while I fell to pieces in disbelief. It had been hours since a bomb dropped on our marriage. "Seriously, get over it! It was only one night! I had too much to drink!" He should have stopped! I wanted to explode. I wanted to scream and punch. Our children were in the next room. My husband used his condescendingly calm voice while blaming my "friend." "She was caressing my penis," under the bubbles of the hot tub while seventeen neighbors mingled watching the night unfold under the lights and sounds of *Boogie Nights*. My mind screamed *what were you doing in a hot tub with her? Why didn't you just get out?* My spouse became the night's entertainment following his caressor into the pool then groped her augmented breasts while I was home in bed trusting him after making love earlier that afternoon. I discovered that my friend, and my life partner left the party together for an unexplained period of time. My head was swimming. Thirty-six hours of crying secretly was exhausting. "Lori, you are so jealous! You are being ridiculous! You are too insecure! You know I love you! I told her that I was never going to leave you!" he professed. All just words. Offensive. Gaslighting. This was not his first indiscretion. He could not be trusted.

I was told to "get over it!" many times in my marriage by my husband and his parents. Often I did just as they said; like turning off a light switch. I dishonored myself. My feelings were disregarded and inconvenient to the people who professed to love me. I loved my family much more than I hated my husband's behavior. What would it take for him to change his ways? Pornography, alcohol, and thousands of hours of playing violent video games infected his brain impeding his ability to see himself or his life clearly.

On a work holiday in Puerto Rico, he groped my friend's breasts as soon as her husband walked away. He felt entitled claiming it to be an "innocent mistake" while laughing "I just had to see." My mind screamed, *YOU SEE WITH YOUR EYES! NOT YOUR HANDS!* It devastated me while I quickly apologized and made excuses. She was embarrassed. It changed everything. Vows of love and trust were broken more times by dishonoring others, which led me to feel ashamed of the man I chose to love. He was inappropriate with more friends over the years grabbing their bums claiming it to be "all in good fun," or "I couldn't help myself." Years of contention existed between my best friend and I because I rejected her when she shared that my husband had placed his hands between her legs. I knew deep down that it was most likely true because he just couldn't seem to help himself, and would come up "playfully" from behind in public to grope me for all the world to see. I felt uncomfortable while convincing myself that he was showing me "love." We all went along with it. There didn't seem to be another choice. "Get over it!"

I was called "crazy" and "irrational" for having a voice. Somehow along the way, I had been programmed to accept when another makes me uncomfortable, I carried the shame and the blame. I was mortified making excuses for my husband's violations. There was too much to "just get over it." I was discomposed.

My spouse was aggravated. He walked by me, certain to make eye contact. His eyes were angry. His words were cold, "You are really crazy, you know that?" I stood observing him opening the fridge and cupboard to pour himself a drink after he promised hours earlier to never drink again. *He called me crazy?* My partner picked up four Advil Cold and Sinus, popping them into his mouth, and washed them down with his stiffly poured drink, all while carrying his forty ounce bottle of Ron Zacapa under his arm down the steep stairs to his man cave. He left me crying in the kitchen claiming his recent "concussion" was causing him head-aches, so he needed to "kill the Germans" to feel better, making certain to mock my heritage. His opening of the Coke, the simple sound I heard thousands of times in my life, set me off. My trau-matized brain took me back to a time and place I did not want to go. I was triggered by detecting familiarity. PTSD set in like damp cold air on arthritic joints. No words escaped me. I was choking on my rapid breaths. Gunfire erupted from the TV downstairs. His swearing at the screen was loud and clear. "JESUS CHRIST YOU FUCKING IDIOT!" into his microphone distracting him for over seven thousand hours at this time in our relationship, where he dominated in a pretend world. Gaming statistics were prioritized over being a partner and parent.

Betrayal unlocked memories that flooded me, drowning my ability to press stop. Scenes played out in fast forward movie clips slowing down enough for my eyes to see and my heart to feel the realness of the moments. Trauma bears no timeframe. Time does not heal. Skin has memories. My skin turned cool and clammy with my heart pounding against my chest wall, knocking as if it wanted to escape. This wasn't a horror movie. It was my life. Visions of my mom and dad laying lifeless, wanting death over being parents to us three children was the opening scene. Both were forced to live roles, responsibilities, and places neither wished to be. We felt that resentment for years. I was four at the time witnessing my parents' attempts to escape it all. Affairs. Alcohol. Drugs. Confusion. Con-tention. Lies. Mental illness. Screaming. Secrets. Strangers were my world from as long as I can remember until the day I left home. Only to find it again in my marriage. A cycle. My known hell.

Dad drank himself stupid most nights with mom eventually following his lead after years of living through disappointments. I witnessed mental illness claim my mom, dad, and brother. Even-tually darkness claimed me. A voice inside my head that told me *I deserved the life I had. It was my fault. I was ugly. I was a bad person. I was not enough. I was evil.*

My middle brother did not recover after losing two childhood friends. One to drowning and the other to a crushing accident. By age fifteen, he was his father's son: drinking to get drunk just like his role model. No good came into our world. My fifth birthday was forgotten because my brother was sick in his "brain," diagnosed with labels that disabled his life. Drugs and dosages were a guessing game. Treatments were experiments. It ruined lives, leading to my brother's addiction to cocaine and codeine. My life was filled with illness and worry. I never knew what I would get. Three people I loved had multiple personalities depending on the drug, dose, and disposition that day. By age fourteen, I was sexually abused by three men in my own home. My father was one of those men that had "too much to drink." That was his normal. He didn't know what he was doing when he climbed into my bed, naked, doing, and telling me things no little girl should experience or hear from any man. Eventually, dad discarded our family when I was fifteen. It was no surprise after walking in on him in my bed with mom's best friend on my thirteenth birthday. Very little survived the fallout of dad's affair. After twenty-five years, dad had not changed as mom hoped. I dreamed of a sober, protective father who would play catch with me. That was never to be. The rest I can't describe. It was an awful moment in time that took years of therapy to package away. Recovery of all the memories released unwanted emotions. Turmoil. The most important men in my life violated love and trust. My father hurt people with his drinking. My husband hurt people with his insatiable ego and sense of entitlement. They both blamed alcohol for their problems. At thirty-eight, it was time for my husband to change. It was time for me to change. The head of our household needed to be healthy to protect our family from threats rather than be the threat. Feeling safe and secure was impossible.

My brain continued playing the hurt and pain caused by men that drunkenly found their way to my bedroom when I was a child. My innocence taken underneath my pink canopy bed. The unwanted touches of men. The unwanted touches from my husband. My brain was going back and forth, unable to discern time while my body remembered everything as if it just happened. The nights of waking up to my husband's boozy breath breathing down my back while he lubricated then inserted himself into me. His intoxication did not sway his level of entitlement that was dangerously high for him to believe that a sleeping wife was consent enough. I carried the burden and responsibility while he carried on like it was nothing. I was his property, not a valued partner. My mind led me to imagine the unthinkable, our daughter was so sweet, innocent, and loved her daddy just like me. The images stopped. I shut them down in my brain by screaming so loud that I didn't recognize myself. The shock of my voice snapped me out of the trance. My german shepherd rushed to my side instantly calming me, while I stroked her majestic fur, laying crumpled side by side on the hardwood floor. Normally, I could minimize my PTSD with techniques learned in therapy: deep breathing, EMDR, and EFT. Betrayal has a certain feel, taste, and smell so pungent it caught me off guard.

After six hours, my husband surfaced from his cave pleading for me to forgive, his breath heavy with booze and eyes glazed over. This was my breaking point. I understood the rules of life. Gramma's wise voice played in my mind, "People that lie and cheat in their most valued relationships will lie and cheat in all aspects of life." My husband was no exception with his wandering eyes and wandering hands revealing his deceitful heart. He made many promises to change. None of them he kept. Seven more years I forgave, offered grace, and gave my whole heart to make our marriage mature, believing love would change him. I made excuses, drank down my dismay and lived in fear of further betrayal. Fear of my daughter being exposed to horny, handsy men that had too much to drink. Hyper vigilance became me.

Eventually our marriage became a cliché with my husband discarding us to find his own happiness with his twelve years younger employee and follow Pearl Jam on tour. He left our two teens in tears and confusion. He declared, "I know it is really selfish, but this is what I really, really want. I want to live my life for me, do what I want to do, date who I want to date. My mom and dad bought me a house with all the amenities I want," with a smirk on his face sounding more like a spoiled toddler than a married man. Twenty years together terminated. He was taken by the woman that he complained "dressed like a whore" at work. Again, my Gramma's voice resounded in my mind, "any man that can be taken is not worth having." My spouse's callous, boastful words to friends, very revealing, "I sleep just fine at night" and "I am happy," while our children and I cried ourselves to sleep for weeks in pain and disbelief that the man we loved and depended on would be so horrendously selfish.

As painful as divorce was, it was a gift freeing me from a man that had no rectitude, respect, regard, or empathy for me or our little family. It forced me to face my many demons and learn hard life lessons, sparking a fire in me to get involved with children at risk and unfortunate ones that have been violated. Experiencing abuse at the hands of men holding power and trust fuelled me to take a stand. Never waste pain!

Our world is experiencing a mental illness epidemic. A sickness called Narcissism. Human trafficking is the product of people that feel entitled to use and discard others for their own personal gain. My experiences with trauma gave me purpose to get involved with Destiny Rescue and Mighty Oaks Global Initiatives because ALL children should be protected from being violated.

"Pornography perpetuates human trafficking, incentivizing the use of children in the pornography industry and human trafficking in order to draw a larger profit."
-Everaccountable.com

"As long as America's men are being trained to think that violent, disturbing pornography is sexually acceptable, an enormous clientele for sex traffickers is being created every day in homes, college dorms, and apartments across the nation."
-John-Henry Westen

* * *

NARCISSIST PERSONALITY DISORDER: THE FIRST SIGN OF ABUSE IS CONFUSION

Most people demonstrate some narcissistic traits on occasion. Men are at higher risk of expressing narcissistic traits. A person with narcissistic personality disorder (NDP) has a consistent pattern of thinking, behaviors, traits, and coping skills that impacts others in negative ways. They can be very charming while they lure you into their life. They strategize and manipulate to get what they want often using fear, privilege, and romance as a motivator. They require a constant supply/source of energy (person)(s) to feed their fragile ego with attention, praise, compliments, awards, sex, and support which makes them feel powerful.

These are some patterns of thinking, behaviors, traits, and coping skills of narcissistic personality disorder:

- lack of empathy/selective empathy
- boundary violator; rules don't apply; above it all
- exploits/shows disregard for others without guilt, remorse or shame
- carries a sense of entitlement and superiority: believe they are elite, deserving of preferential treatment; grandiose
- lives in a fantasy world that supports their delusions of grandeur (video games, pornography)
- expect others to make them happy and will discard/replace when that is no longer achieved
- arrogant, abrasive, aggressive, arbitrary, argumentative, boastful, pretentious
- egotistical, opinionated, intense, inauthentic
- charismatic, charming (uses flattery), conceited, controlling, nervy, flirty, seductive
- exaggerated need for attention, admiration, and validation
- compulsively makes inappropriate comments, no filter
- addicted to power, prestige, sex, image, and will take credit that is not earned

- public perception is important, therefore, some are society's "philanthropists" that use giving as a marketing tool Eg. having rooms, programs, schools, or hospital equipment named after themselves
- competitive, win at all costs mentality, ungracious winner and sore loser
- poor listening skills, unless they will benefit from the exchange
- serial romantic that put certain people that feed their insatiable demands and ego on a pedestal
- sarcasm and belittling others is a preferred form of humor
- hyper critical and hypersensitive
- more likely to cheat in relationships and life
- difficulty communicating effectively at home, work, and as part of a team
- fakes or creates health issues to keep attention on them as a form of control/power
- displays moodiness, brooding, and depression when others do not show full appreciation for their "specialness"
- uses condescending and derogatory language
- lives for awards, rewards, and recognition
- avoids accountability for mistakes by blaming, denying, and deflecting
- manipulative
- compulsive lying

A person that has NPD will discard their partner/spouse/family after they have their new "supply" lined up (usually a coworker/employee). The new "supply" will be younger, money driven, and attracted to charm, power, position, prestige, and privilege. The narcissist love bombs the new supply and shares a false narrative that their current relationship is over, their partner is crazy, controlling, abusive, irrational, they grew apart or are no longer in love/friends/associates (if in a professional situation). The narcissistic person and new supply miraculously have everything in common. The devaluation and discard of their current relationship/spouse/

family began the moment the new supply gave the NPD the attention, validation, and admiration they demand. The NPD will create confusion in their current commitment/marriage/partnership by using contempt, criticism, and defensiveness with blows of indifference then words like "true love," "perfect partner," "soulmate," "forever," and "one and only" to further confuse, reassure and distract the soon to be dissolved partnership. Narcissistic people plan and strategize using their fans/enablers to support them. They are takers, seldom feeling remorse, more likely justified. Parenting is of no real interest or consequence. Escaping to a new relationship is key. They don't care if they set off bombs in other people's lives because they never truly loved. Commitment is inconvenient. Love is purely a selfish, self serving endeavour for a narcissist. It is all about how a person caters to their needs or makes their life easier/better. Narcissistic people will walk away from responsibilities leaving damage in their wake. They feel entitled to seek happiness at the expense of their spouse, children, and family. The cycle repeats when the narcissist is no longer happy or becomes bored. It isn't personal. People are used for their pleasure and service to be discarded at their whim. Unfortunately, narcissistic people do not change. They do not reflect on how their words, actions, and behaviors impact others because they only think of themselves and having their own way. People are easily replaced and they feel vindicated in their toxic ways.

For this world to thrive, we must create a
state of compassion and empathy for all living
beings because when one suffers, we all suffer.

CHAPTER SEVEN

Let It GO!

*"Healing is layers. Healing is time.
Healing is excruciating. Healing is ugly.
Healing is surprising. Once you think it's
done, it's not."*

CHARLEYNE OULTON

CHARLEYNE OULTON

Charleyne is a confident, happy, mom of three children who lives on beautiful Vancouver Island, BC. She is genuine, experienced, and passionate about creating and maintaining a life full of grace and joy. She is a member of the Royal Canadian Navy, an appreciated health and wellness coach, and an award-winning author even through the busy and beautiful chaos of raising a family. It is her purpose to inspire women, and specifically the busy, overworked, and exhausted mothers around the world, to remember their personal strength and that they, along with us all, are deserving of a life filled with health, happiness, and harmony.

www.coachcharleybrown.com
ig: @coachcharley.brown | fb: @coachcharleybrown
#coachcharleybrown | goodreads: charleyne oulton

*I will remember and recover,
not forgive and forget.*

For over one hundred years, parents have been encouraging and allowing their children to take part in Boy Scouts Canada in order to explore their capabilities, develop confidence, and build friendships. Parents have been entrusting this popular organization with their children's health and safety. However, parents are now expressing grave questions and concerns, worrying that their children are not being protected from sexual predators, after a disturbing and shocking documentary produced by *The Fifth Estate* on CBC News[1] aired on television.

An investigation led by the *Los Angeles Times* and *The Fifth Estate* uncovered that for decades, Scouts Canada kept a list of volunteers: *A confidential list* of known men ejected from the institution for sexual misconduct or concerns about sexual abuse. This documentary focused primarily on one man, a Canadian convicted of molesting young scouts in the United States throughout the 1970s and '80s. This known offender was able to volunteer for the Scouts in Canada after his release from a California mental facility.

In 1975, this man allegedly made his way in a stolen car from British Columbia to California. An eleven-year-old Canadian child living in California was kidnapped and strapped into a small stolen airplane: a new special friend for this offender. But when the level of the fuel tank suddenly dropped, the plane was forced to do an emergency landing and the child was returned home after being tracked down by the police.

There was *not* a background investigation on the known offender, and thus the abuse continued when he became a Scouts

---

1   CBC News. 2011. "Scouts failed to stop a sexal predator: CBC investigation."
https://www.cbc.ca/news/canada/scouts-failed-to-stop-sexual-predator-cbc-investigation-1.1043966

leader. Throughout the 1970s and '80s, the same man was involved with the Scouts across California and British Columbia, molesting at least eight more scouts.

By August of 1979, the known offender had returned to the Victoria, British Columbia area and within a few years, unfortunately began to lead a local scout troop.

In 1988, he was sentenced to thirty days in jail and banned from associating with youth groups such as Scouts, YMCA, and little league after assaulting yet another young child at a public swimming pool.

However, it was not until 1995 that police began their first large-scale investigation involving this man, after a tip came in from a very concerned girlfriend of his: *my mother.* It was sixteen years after the Boy Scouts of America created a "Perversion File" on this man and nearly a decade after Canadian Scout authorities put him on their confidential list.

In 1996, he was again convicted of sexually abusing children; this time, he was declared a dangerous offender, a designation reserved for Canada's most violent criminals and sexual predators. Three of these convictions were for abuse of former boy scouts, and later he admitted to having at least a dozen victims.

* * *

This was my special friend.

My friend with whom I had secrets.

My friend who told me our secrets would hurt my family.

* * *

He shamed and insulted me into believing that if I spoke of our secret, my family would disown me. Only as an adult did I realize that this friend was actually a sexual predator who was grooming and training me and my family, most likely from the day we met.

In the beginning of our friendship, he appeared caring, attentive, genuine, and very loving. He was charming, in fact. My mom and I were blind and did not see that this kindness was fake, and was being used to win over our trust and confidence. He quickly became the one who tucked me in at night, even though my innocent yet strong instinct told me I did not want him to do it. Although

I appreciated the cuddle and story before going to sleep, I did not like when he would lift the covers and quickly slide beneath them. He was never awaiting my permission: he knew his intention, and there was no interrupting him. He would pull me close to him and rub my hair, and his hand would wander down my arm and usually land on my tummy. I told myself to lie very still and be silent. His breath would quicken and become shallow, and his eyes would close. I would feel something very hard begin to poke at my side, and I would remain frozen and motionless, with my eyes squeezed shut as tightly as possible, hoping he would just leave. Eventually he would slip out of my bed, kissing the top of my head, tuck in the blankets all around me, way too tight, and tiptoe out of the room.

The moment he left the room, I would sit up in my bed, trembling, untuck all of my blankets, and start calling out to my mom. At this point I usually went to my mom, who was frustrated I was up again and she would send me back to my room. It's not her fault that she was being short with me. She had worked a long day and was exhausted and she had no idea what was happening. But when she came to tuck me back in and snuggle me safely, with my twenty teddies, and yellow knit blankie, I could finally slip away into sleep.

* * *

My mother was persuaded to allow me to go on a trip and this was organized for just me and him. With both my parents' permission, we loaded into his semi-truck (he was a commercial truck driver) and started on our way to Vancouver, British Columbia. We were scheduled to do one delivery and one pickup, and then we were to enjoy a popular arcade-restaurant. Unfortunately he had other plans and turned toward Washington State. He took me over the U.S. border without my family's consent, knowledge, or proper paperwork, and without notifying Canadian Border Services (CBA). I was only nine years old.

As we approached the border crossing, he told me to get comfy, and hide in the back of the truck under some bedding and to quietly read a book. He told me that this would save him money; I did not understand what was happening or that it was wrong. So I whispered, "Yes" and obeyed: what else could I do? I did not know that he was kidnapping me, that I was leaving Canada. I chose to *behave* and listen to him. I did not want him to get angry with me.

Once we got through the border crossing, he made a stop at a nearby store. He turned on his charisma and charm, gifting me with snacks, and pop, and whatever else I wanted. He was being very generous. "What a good little girl," he stated as he put his arm around my shoulder and gave me a squeeze while we stood in line at the store. I did not realize that he was trying to rebuild my trust in him and keep my devotion strong. I just felt like the luckiest girl on the planet.

I was so naïve.

I did not have enough life experience to know that you do not get expensive gifts from an abuser because they think you are awesome. The reason they gift you something is because they are trying to manipulate and control you into thinking *they* are awesome. He was gifting me out of fear and out of necessity to keep me happy and calm.

He abused me that night in the back of his truck for the first time, and on many other nights during that trip. He exploited my vulnerability. He molested me. I was more tired than I ever remember. Sapped of energy. Will. Joy. All gone.

But above all else, I wanted my dad and I wanted my mom.

To be home, to have a very long bath, and to cuddle my cat, my blankie, and my favorite stuffed parrot, Perry. Even though I wanted to not exist, to collapse into the bedding and just decay, I had a deep gut instinct to call my mom. I did not know what she would say, but I asked to stop at the next gas station to use the bathroom, and while he was getting fuel, I begged the attendant to let me use their phone, saying it was an emergency.

There wasn't anything to do except sit there and breathe, sit there while my heart continued to pump blood through my body, and feel thankful that my mom answered my call. I cannot remember what I said to her; I did not confess my secrets, but through my undertone and her own maternal instincts, she understood it was an emergency and that I needed to return home immediately.

When I arrived back to my mom, without him, I did not disclose to her what had happened. I pretended that everything was okay, even though I knew in my soul it was not. I pretended for a very long time. I tried to live my life the way it had been before.

When a child is abused by a parent or someone with a parental role, they tend to have mixed feelings about the abuser. In a way, I missed him once I returned home, as I never saw him again. I missed his praise and attention; however, I did not miss how uncomfortable he made me feel.

I felt perpetually dirty, no matter how many bubble baths I took. I developed a fear of the night and the dark; I hated sleeping alone, being alone with my thoughts and memories. No matter how hard I tried, I struggled to settle into a restful sleep. I was too young to know that sexual assault survivors often experience sleepless nights or suffer from night terrors. It was when I slept that the ugly flashbacks and memories surfaced and startled me awake.

Could people tell I had been raped? Was I
visibly flawed now? Did I look different?

I eventually caved and told my friend a little bit of my truth while we played with our dolls at her house. I feel grateful that she told her mom after I left; her mom called mine, and my mom sat me down to talk to me. Within an hour, I had unleashed my tormented experiences and my mom instantly called the police. A few days later, she and I met with the police and with a counselor from Victim Services. This caused many flashbacks for me, as it had been much easier for me to forget about what happened than to talk about it in specific detail. As I described what happened, I would break a sweat, tremble, and feel very anxious.

I was vulnerable, impressionable, and a shy child when my trauma began. Every single painful detail is etched in my memory. My nostrils seem to be filled with his musky aftershave and stale cigarette smell. I cannot seem to forget the scratchy sound of his boxers being pulled down while he wiggled under our sleeping bag. The uncomfortable sexual games, fondling, cuddling, and being told that we had to sleep in the nude together to keep our bodies warm in the back of his semi-truck continually replay in my mind. I can vividly remember the thumping sound of my racing heartbeat, like a deafening drum, as I sat in a room talking to a grief counselor about my abuse. I remember feeling incredibly annoyed. I had been clean, I had been a child. I hated all the questions, conflict, and drama that my life had become, all because an adult man made a bad decision with a vulnerable child.

OUR CASE EXPLODED

My name was protected because I was a juvenile, but as my story made it to various news stations, my mom was interviewed numerous times. This inspired other adults who had also been victims of this man to stand together with me, and bravely face their ugly past as well. My mom made it her life mission to make sure this man suffered for what he had done. And I chose to no longer be silent: I chose to share my truth, even with the courts, and a trial date was set.

Recovering from sexual assault takes time. The healing process can be raw, uncomfortable, and emotionally painful. I needed to learn that it was possible to regain my sense of control, rebuild my self-worth, and heal.

Sexual violence is shockingly common in our society: according to the Centers for Disease Control and Prevention (CDC), nearly one in five women are raped or sexually assaulted at some point in their lives, often by someone they know and trust.[2] These gross statistics are not limited to women; men and boys also suffer rape and sexual trauma each year.

Regardless of age or gender, the impact of sexual violence goes far beyond any physical injuries. The mental and emotional scars are often more damaging than the physical abuse itself. The trauma of being sexually assaulted can be earth-shattering, leaving the survivor feeling humiliated, scared, isolated, ashamed, or plagued by nightmares, flashbacks, and other unpleasant or undesirable memories. Often one feels victimized and unsure of where or whom to turn to, and instead turn inwards; one then falls victim to the same predator through the shame and fear of bringing the assault into the real world by verbalizing it.

After my trauma, the world did not feel like a safe place anymore. I no longer trusted others. I did not even trust myself. You

2   Newser. 2014. "CDC: 1 in 5 Women Are Rape Victims." https://www.newser.com/story/193520/cdc-1-in-5-women-are-rape-victims.html

may be able to relate. Have you ever questioned your judgment, your self-worth, and even your sanity? Blaming yourself for what catastrophic event has happened, or believed that you're "dirty," disgusting, or damaged goods? Often after sexual trauma, relationships feel dangerous, and intimacy impossible. On top of that, like many trauma survivors, you may struggle with Post Traumatic Stress Disorder (PTSD), Anxiety, and Depression.

Childhood trauma can affect a person so greatly because of its presence during an important time of development. Events become embedded in every fiber of one's identity as a child. This time of life is so crucial to your entire future. This is the unique nature of Complex Post Traumatic Stress Disorders (C-PTSD), which I was diagnosed with later in life. This form of PTSD results from repeated trauma over months or years, rather than a single event. C-PTSD doesn't merely change a person: it creates them, and sometimes defines their entire life. It builds one's every trait, interest, and understanding of the world, with this toxin as it courses through their veins. Nothing is unaffected or unaltered because the trauma created all there is to alter. Moving forward does not mean moving back to before the trauma; it is in every essence a rebirth, renewal, and re-education of life itself. To move on, we cannot erase because to erase the effect of our traumas, we in theory erase ourselves. However, we can redefine ourselves, recreate our image, and grow strong through the memory and understanding of what happened to us.

Healing is layers. Healing is time.
Healing is excruciating. Healing is ugly.
Healing is surprising. Once you think it's done,
it's not.

At the time of my questioning, I was a young child ignorant of sex, molestation, and even the simplest thing like what an erection was. They placed me on the stand in front of my family, the predator, and many strangers all looking at me as if I were lying. But I tried my absolute best to defend myself against all the inevitable questions of rape culture: the things victims get asked because society's first instinct seems to be to examine the victim's outfit, behavior, and deportment instead of the abuser's. I tried to be strong.

I do not know how many minutes or hours passed as I sat beside the Judge, but I remember feeling oddly calm and numb. This is a shock response and is often misunderstood. Maybe others viewed me as having tremendous control or as being okay, but I was not. I believed that it was all my fault for not resisting him more forcefully. I felt as if I had done something wrong and had somehow caused this to happen to me. I felt as if they forced me to endure a lifetime of pain and shame for what had happened.

For so long, I had wanted to have an actual conversation with the Judge about what had transpired between *him* and me, but this was obviously never going to happen. What I had been craving was a resolution, a peace summit, from which I could emerge healthy, healed, and happy. Unfortunately, I feel the courts failed me. I was tricked, and manipulated into answering questions that I did not understand, and I feel they took advantage of me. I was confused and didn't answer their questions how they wanted me to.

I now realize that everything I was feeling was a typical reaction to trauma. Helplessness, shame, being unclean, suffering PTSD and anxiety, and feeling defective are all very common for those who survive sexual trauma and rape. Regardless of your age or gender, it can be extraordinarily difficult to admit that you suffered sexual trauma, rape, and abuse.

Typically victims believe their abuse was deserved and meaningful because it's less scary to be in a position where you've been rightfully punished for something, than it is to acknowledge you have to live in a world with predators who will hurt you merely for amusement and for their own pleasure.

I couldn't have endured it, had I known as a child that I was at the mercy of a predator who would harm me for fun. How would any child victim of abuse cope with that? How would we live knowing that pain and suffering are waiting for us no matter what we do? Realizing that some punishments have no connection to our mistakes, that they can occur randomly at our abuser's will? Knowing that we are forced to live amongst people who cause us pain just because they could, because it felt good to them, and we can't stop them from hurting us no matter what? This knowledge alone is lethal. No child can bear living in an environment of hatred, neglect, and meaningless pain. We have to believe there is love, we have to believe there are good intentions, we have to believe it is connected to our actions or that it is our fault: otherwise we would have no reason, no hope to continue living. When we blame ourselves and absolve them of guilt, we are just clinging to life.

It's incredibly hard to change this mindset because it goes against our primal instincts, which warn us from deep inside that accepting this reality might cost us our lives. Recovering from this mindset means reconstructing our entire reality. It means accepting that it cannot be okay to expose us to this kind of struggle. It cannot be okay to push us this far.

There is a stigma that comes with the label of sexual assault victim. It seems easier to pretend it never happened and to keep it a secret. But if you stay silent it can happen to others, by the same abuser. You also deny yourself the help you need, isolating you from your support network, and from the opportunity to regain your strength. It is very hard to heal if you avoid the truth.

Set yourself free from useless suffering. Let it go.
You deserve to heal and live a life full of joy.

I did not bring the assault on myself because of something I wore, said, or did. I do not question myself for trusting him or judge myself for freezing when he abused me. There is nothing I can do to change the past. *IT* happened.

I can, however, choose my thoughts and reactions. As an adult, I now choose to forgive him. I choose to let it go, but to share my trauma with others and offer them love and support, and a listening ear. This is my power: the ability to take my rape and turn it into something good. Everything that happens has a reason, purpose, and difference that it will make. I strongly believe that my trauma happened, so that I could relate to and support others who have suffered trauma. I choose to take the bad that happened to me and make it the good that I spread with the world.

One way I do that is by sharing my healing journey. It is a journey that continues for me every day, and if you are a fellow survivor, it will for you as well. Every day, try your best to think of yourself as improving into the best version of yourself. Remember to care for your mental, emotional, and physical needs; don't push yourself too far or run yourself ragged and make sure to take breaks and time for yourself.

FIVE THINGS I DO EVERY DAY THAT HELP ME HEAL:

1. Walk Outside.

I crave nature like others crave sugar or sex. So I carve out time every single day to be outside, over and above my day-to-day schedule and routine. Sometimes this is with my dog, my kids, my spouse, or even alone. Exercising in nature boosts my mood, increases my energy, flushes my body and mind of toxins, and manages my stress. Spending time outside is a natural antidepressant that I truly recommend. You can often find me barefoot and hugging trees.

2. Practice Gratitude Journaling.

This is where I realize and remind myself of my abundance! Writing has always been one of the main tools I use to cope with and manage my anxiety, and heal from my trauma. When my mind is garbled with too much garbage and my head feels like it's going to explode, I can sort out my thoughts and feelings just by journaling and drawing mind maps. I've even written in the sand with a stick out of desperation to stop my negative thoughts from spiraling out of control and to make tangible sense of them. Journaling, doodling, and writing also help me stay on track and reach my goals, while letting me emotionally heal, clarify, and realize what is really bothering me. I can then choose my response to feelings, thoughts, and situations.

3. Commit a random act of Kindness, daily.

Have you ever heard the quote, *"One kind word can change someone's entire day"*? I love everything about this quote. You and I truly harbor the ability to make someone's day a little easier, to help them smile! Lend someone a helping hand every day. Throw kindness around like confetti! Try it!

4. Meditate and Pray.

Prayer and meditation help me release my burdens and calm my spirit. I encourage you to learn to control your thoughts, and become a master of your thoughts and mind. Practicing awareness has helped me get more in touch with life's uncomfortable feelings and moments, and learn to be more calm and more focused. This then allows me to pay attention to my thoughts without allowing them to hold me down. It is hard to learn something new, so remember to be patient as you learn to wander and navigate through your mind, with all its spiraling thoughts. Any and all spiritual practices help me heal.

5. With all your Soul, let go and attempt to forgive.

Go on with your life. Let go of the past! From my own experiences, I have learned that you cannot live both in the past and in the present. They are very different realities. You cannot have absolute hatred for an individual or experience and still forgive them. At times, forgiveness can feel impossible. It's like the Rubik's Cube of the soul. But it's worth the effort because forgiveness equates to freedom. Freedom from feeling the torture again, and again, and again. The purpose of my life is to be happy and healthy while realizing my worth and blessings and to continually share my knowledge with others. It is impossible to be both positive and negative at the very same moment. The emotions do not marry. I have taught myself how to let go of the past, the past trauma, pain, and angst, without forgetting about it. My past experiences have helped shape me into the woman I am today, and so I honor those experiences, both positive and negative. But I also use meditation and prayer to help me reflect on those feelings, lessons, and moments, and move past them by building new patterns and habits that are healthy and help me feel joy.

* * *

You may also consider joining a support group for sexual abuse survivors. Support groups can even be anonymous and in my opinion, they help you feel less isolated and provide invaluable information on how to cope with your symptoms and work toward recovery.

It takes a level of self-love, dedication, and determination to live your greatest life. You must look within, at every area of your life, and ask yourself these questions: *Am I on course? Am I growing mentally, emotionally, and spiritually?* Anything that is blocking you from living your greatest life, make the tough decision to let go. This includes trauma. LET IT GO!

If you can relate to my story and are reading these words, CONGRATULATIONS! You survived another day today and because of that, I am proud of you. I know it can be very hard sometimes. When there are days you feel like you just cannot go further, remember that you made it through today and all the days you've overthought. The journey to recovery is about reclaiming your power, rediscovering who you are, what makes you happy and what kind of life you want to live. Am I fully healed? NO! Not at all. But I have learned that trauma is an opportunity for growth and for massive transformations. For that I am grateful. One of the most important things I have learned in my life is that our greatest pains are in fact our greatest gifts.

I hope that you get lots of rest for another adventurous day ahead with pure love and light: you are, and will always be, a divine blessing.

Much Love,
Charleyne Oulton
#coachcharleybrown

STOLEN INNOCENCE

Courtney Battie

September 18th, 2019 was a day like any other, there was no foreseeing that this particular day would change my life completely. A friend of mine who I had known for five years at the time stopped by to see how I was doing; I opened the door to him and he stepped inside my home. After a quick visit he proceeded to push me and sexually assault me . . . despite my strong attempts to fight him off and repeatedly saying *"NO!"*

I was mortified. Hurt. Scared. It took me over twenty-four hours to come up with the courage to phone the police after receiving yet another text message of apology from him. One week after my attack, I made the official report and pressed charges against him. He was arrested that night. It was an emotional rollercoaster; I struggled with feeling that I could have done more to stop him, or I should have reported him sooner. My mind raced with anxiety, fear, and thoughts such as *why me?*

Don't let trauma limit you, or control your life!

Pressing charges was not an option for myself and for my girls I wanted to demonstrate strength to my daughters that this behaviour is never okay. NO means NO! After going to the Police, I realized I had to talk to my daughters; that was one of the hardest conversations I have ever had with them. I explained to them my trauma, but spared some of the gruesome details of what happened so they could understand my behaviour; the sleepless nights; the constant anxiety; the mood swings.

Recovering from a sexual assault is extremly hard, I frequently see him driving on the highway; I have not had a good sleep since the attack; I still suffer from flashbacks and anxiety. I started talking with a counselor to help me deal with the trauma, I feel like this has helped me get everything out in the open. Writing and journaling has helped me work through the strong emotions I suffer since my trauma. I am grateful for the friends who have supported me, answered my calls, texts, hugged me while I cried. I am trying to grow, heal, and gain mental strength. I fully realize I'm only a victim if I allow myself to be a victim. I started taking my dog,

Beau, for more walks which helps me clear my head, refocus my thoughts, and face my anxiety. Being outside has assisted me to think clearly and feel present in the moment again.

I want women who have suffered the same abuse to know that they are strong enough to overcome their trauma and strong enough to press charges against their accuser, even though it will be hard and terrifying. Since coming forward with my truth, a huge weight has been lifted off my shoulders and I have begun my lengthy healing process. Being sexually assaulted has changed who I was, but it is not who I am. I now view the world differently. It makes me mad that this happened to me and terrified that traumas continue to happen all around the world every day. Why did he choose to ruin our friendship over this? I may never find out the answer.

I want women to remember their worth. I am here to remind YOU, that YOU are not alone! You did not deserve this! You did not cause this! And that you are brave enough to come forward, just like I have. I am determined to not let this hurt me anymore. I am a survivor and I am strong.

CHAPTER EIGHT

The Great Escape

"Leaving isn't always giving up or running away. Sometimes it is simply standing up for and saving yourself."

LINDSAY WHITHAM

Lindsay Whitham is a free spirit and an old soul. As the single mother of three precious children, Lindsay is guided by a strong sense to be a good role model. She values experiences over material possessions and hopes to pass this love for learning and exploration onto her children.

Lindsay is an animal lover. She has an undeniable passion for horses, evident from early childhood, and the magnificent four-legged souls remain a steady constant in her life today. Though Lindsay was born and raised just north of Toronto, her heart has always been called to nature and all of its wonders. Being able to experience wildlife in its natural habitat brings Lindsay great joy.

From a young age, Lindsay was known for being wise beyond her years. A strong academic, Lindsay excelled in all studies, particularly maths and sciences. Pursuing childhood dreams, she graduated high school with honours and went on to study Animal Biology at the University of Guelph. Partway through her studies she had a change of heart and stepped away, later receiving a business diploma with honours.

Although Lindsay has dabbled with different employment options, as well as some entrepreneurial endeavours, she is working at discovering her true calling.

Lindsay is strong, reliable, genuine, and loyal to a fault. Her empathetic nature tends to attract challenging situations, but she knows they play an important role in her personal growth. Having driven across Canada, from coast to coast, Lindsay highly recommends the experience. Pictures simply don't do the Canadian landscape justice.

ig: @spiritedbynature

It's funny how we grow up with a plan in our heads. A plan of how we think life *should* be, the things we think we *should* achieve. The way we *should* feel. Yet, no matter how much we think we have it figured out, our entire plan can crumble in what feels like a moment. We can be left trying to put the pieces back together, not knowing what the puzzle is supposed to look like to begin with.

Growing up, I was constantly told how smart I was and that I could achieve whatever I set my mind to. And yet, here I am, divorced, mother of three kids, working a low paying job. I have limited time for sleep, never mind time for fun or romance. I, the straight A student who had the world at her fingertips, ended up here.

Now, before you close your eyes and dread the pain of the rest of my story, I want to tell you this. My story isn't one of doom and gloom. This is the story of a woman who clung to her master plan for dear life, and as a result, learned a lot of hard lessons along the way. These lessons, I will pass onto you. Why? Because we are not so different, you and I, and we are worth it. This journey I am on is far from done. Life has no destination. But here is what I know for sure. If I can find the courage to break free from the master plan, including the dreams it promised, you can too. My story will grant you permission to free yourself from the shackles that claim your power. Are you ready?

My lifelong dream of being a large animal veterinarian wasn't really what I saw myself doing once I started studying Animal Biology. I had spent my entire life thinking I would follow this career path, but midway through University I realized it wasn't actually what I wanted. Aside from my unwavering needle phobia, I was torn between having a family and having a career as a large animal vet. At that time, I didn't think I could have both. With my mind spinning, I lost much of my drive and direction. It was only a matter of time before my grades started slipping and I decided to drop out. I took a break, hoping to gain some clarity and direction. I worked for a bit, and also got a business diploma at a local college. I figured I could put that to work while I figured things out.

Amidst the derailment of my education and career plan, I decided I may as well work on the *marriage and kids* part of the life plan. A short while later, I met my now ex-husband. Things progressed quickly. It felt as though we had a lot in common. This guy seemed to get me in ways no one else ever had. Long before getting married, we discovered that we shared the same dreams. A house overlooking a creek, with a front porch to sit on. Enjoying each other's company over hot morning beverages. We wanted to grow old and share our whole lives together. Somewhere in there we would get some livestock, do some farming, and have some kids. We were going to live what I thought and hoped would be a simple and happy life. And, for a while, we did these things. We moved to a farm and raised some goats, cows, and dogs. We had fun. We were spontaneous. We travelled. Life was good. Maybe, too good. I remember some friends and family telling me it all seemed too good to be true. Which, as it turned out, was the only truth.

Despite enjoying many of the dreams mentioned above, I left three times before we were even married. The lies, deceit, and cheating would become too much: the hushed phone calls and abrupt hang-ups, "disappearing" texts, and large amounts of money being withdrawn with no trace or reasonable explanation; lies in response to the most simple and unimportant questions; the endless double-standards, including but not limited to, being questioned or punished for not answering his phone call, email, or text—immediately. Though, if I was ever to question a delay or lack of his response, it was completely unacceptable of me—he was "busy" and I had no right to question it. I was skillfully and often passively guilted out of doing things, such as visiting with friends and family or partaking in a hobby. I came to dread being in public together as he took any opportunity to not have to be present (physically or mentally) and it was clear to everyone and embarrassing for me. And yet, each time I returned. Flooded by his apologies, explanations, and reassurance, I dismissed it all as I clung to the dream of having a simple life with this man. I remember standing at the altar, tears running down my face, knowing I was making a huge mistake, but afraid to let everyone down. I was embarrassed. I'd brought all these people together. They'd spent time and money on my wedding. *I couldn't just call it off and run away.*

In hindsight, most of the people in attendance would have fully supported me and my decision. A few may have even cheered as I ran out. But there I stood, in tears, crying the false lashes right off of my face, barely able to recite my vows. I told myself it was just wedding day jitters. It wasn't jitters. It was my gut, my intuition. I ignored it and let my ego win. The, now clearly irrational, self-manifested fear of disappointing others and being embarrassed got the better of me.

It was a long time before I got any better at listening to those nudges. In fact, in the eight years of dating, breaking up, getting married, moving (*oh the moving)*, and having kids, I'd silenced my inner voice completely. I'd lost the ability to trust my own intuition. I'd lost myself.

The day I realized my husband actually believed his own lies was life shattering. To a person who can't lie to save their life, this realization was something I couldn't, and still can't comprehend. *How can someone possibly believe their own lies?* It led me to question everything. *Was any part of this relationship real? Was anything he said or did genuine?* It was a very scary place to be, to realize I had spent almost a decade in a relationship that now felt like a giant fabrication. It's hard to believe another human, especially one you think you love (and thought loved you back) could be so intentionally hurtful; To have no regard for your feelings or wellbeing. Love shouldn't hurt. Love isn't being guilted, outright or implied, into doing things you don't want to for fear of losing that love. Love isn't being threatened when you ask questions about things that don't feel right. And love definitely isn't someone forcing themselves on you while you are pinned, face down on a mattress, *screaming NO!* and *crying* and *pleading* for them to *STOP!* And because I just couldn't wrap my head around the reality coming to light, I would try and rationalize it. I would try to justify the actions, the lies, and the warning signs. Despite having undeniable, hard evidence in hand. I would dismiss everything, believing what he told me, ultimately causing me to lose faith in my own judgement and my own thoughts. *Maybe I really am crazy like he says. Maybe I really am making it up in my own head. Maybe I was the one at fault.*

I felt like a shell of a human being as I arrived at the point where being intimate with my husband made me feel physically ill. It was no longer an act of love, but an obligation, a duty to carry out. And it would often bring me to tears. I hated myself for putting up with it all, for allowing myself to stay stuck in such a mess, for not getting out, breaking free. But I couldn't see a way out. I felt trapped. And truthfully, there were many times I felt that I somehow deserved all of it. That it was somehow my fault. I had lost faith in my ability to be an independent woman. I believed I couldn't make it on my own financially to provide for my children. I believed I didn't deserve any better. I believed I was in love, and maybe this was just what love was going to look like for me. I believed in every single thing, except in myself.

But it wasn't my fault. And I didn't deserve it. No one deserves to be treated like that.

Things would always turn around when he realized how close I was to leaving. Over and over and over, it was a vicious cycle. I believe the term is "hoovering"—sucking you back in. When things got really bad and I mustered up the courage to leave, something really good would miraculously happen. It was a convenient, cyclical tool he used to keep me around. The times I had mustered up the courage to leave and shut him out the hoovering went into overdrive. He knew he could break me down. Showing up where he knew I would be unable to avoid him. Threatening his own suicide. Promising to change, to go to counselling. Whatever it took to get me back. That, and his repeated efforts of what I now know to be nothing more than "love bombing," blurred my vision of reality. And it worked. No matter how far I had made it each time, I would either stay with him or go back to him.

I grew to believe I couldn't have the life I wanted on my own. I couldn't survive on my own. I wasn't enough. I didn't believe I could bring my dreams to life on my own, physically or financially. I thought I needed a man and I thought that man was him. I believed we shared the dream I was so desperately clinging to. I had much of the lifestyle I had always thought I wanted and I was terrified to lose it and never get it back.

It was a wild roller coaster of extreme ups and downs; well played ups and downs. I was weak both physically and mentally. I had little fight left and I was tired. When I would feel some strength, I would start to see through the fog of empty promises. But, by that point, I was convinced I was not loveable. I was not capable, and I was not worthy.

These wounds ran deep and I still, to this day, struggle with the damage. Slowly it is getting better.

I remember a pivotal moment in my journey when I literally saw my future reflecting back at me through a family member. This woman had grown old, and spent a lifetime succumbing to similar abuse to what I was living with. She didn't leave. She stayed. It finally hit me. This is where I was going to end up if I didn't get out. This was going to be me in forty years. The thought terrified me beyond any fear I had felt before. I couldn't imagine living my entire life afraid, unhappy, and powerless. I had to get out.

I didn't know how to get out, but I knew it was time. And this time, I couldn't go back. I had to be strong. I knew it was going to be hard, especially since I was on maternity leave with twins and a two-year-old, and I had no job. I found strength in my children. I wasn't leaving just for me, I wanted a better life for my kids. We all deserved better. They deserved a mother who could be present with them. A mother who could see her own worth and fight for it. They needed a strong role model, not one living in doubt and shame that was constantly walking on eggshells and consumed in self-hatred and disappointment.

It was time to escape. I had to make a plan.

It's hard to cut the strings. It's scary to lose the support you *think* you need. But it's amazing when you realize you don't *need* those strings to stand. You're not a puppet. We all have strengths, sometimes they are hard to see. Start with little, seemingly meaningless things like brushing your hair or teeth, and build as you are able. Write them down if you can as a reminder on the days you feel hopeless. I had to reach back, remember a younger me and her strengths. She was and is still there, even though she feels very lost and even non-existent at times. She did things. And so can you and I.

I rebuilt myself and regained my strength. I started doing more things on my own, stepping out of my comfort zone. I took the kids to mom and tot groups. I ran errands with a two year old and infant twins. Little by little, I learned how to manage life with three small children on my own. It is important to recognize the small victories, because those are the victories that happen each and every day and often go unnoticed. I realized being alone was better than being at war every day. It was better than being angry and resentful. It was better than stressing and wondering and searching for a grain of truth in the mountains of lies. It was better than withering away with someone who didn't value me. It wasn't perfect, but it was better. I'd found my voice.

I had a new plan.

Recently, I participated in a support group for abused women at a local women's interval home. This support was free of charge. Which I feel is so important as many women in these types of situations don't have (access to) the funds to pay for support. Often the abuser controls the money and would find out, putting the victim at more of a risk. Sometimes a woman has already left the situation and is barely getting by financially. The purpose of these programs is to offer a safe community for women. To allow them to truly feel they are not alone. To share information and knowledge, providing the tools to either get out of a bad situation, or learn how to recognize them in the future and steer clear.

I wish I had found this resource sooner. It is scary how commonplace it is to think that if it is not physical abuse, then it's not actually abuse. Or, it's just not *that* serious. It opened my eyes to the effects of abuse and how it had tarnished my ability to think clearly. What a relief to know I wasn't crazy or alone. There are people out there who understand; more people than you can imagine.

I am not sure if mental and emotional abuse are on the rise or if there are simply more people bringing it to light. They do not produce the same visual evidence as physical abuse and therefore are more difficult to attach consequences and perhaps people feel they can get away with this behaviour. The more we talk about it, the more people will be aware and will be able to recognize the signs both in their own lives and in the lives of others. The more light we shed, the less acceptable and commonplace it will be.

Leaving an abusive relationship is not giving up. Leaving an abusive relationship is saving yourself. Leaving is an act of self-love. It's a reminder that you are enough. You are worth it. You deserve better, and *can* do better.

* * *

After getting back on my feet, it was time to start moving forward, to make new plans and find ways to bring them to life. I had to find myself again.

I remembered trips to the cottage as a little girl, waking my dad when it was still dark so we could have breakfast and be down on the dock as the sun came up. We would fish all weekend, keeping track of how many fish we caught and trying to out-fish the other. We had fun and I really enjoyed those moments. I remembered thinking I would need a man to take me fishing. I never thought it would be something I could do on my own. I wanted my children to experience this kind of joy and happiness. I had to make it happen. I rented a cottage where my family used to fish, and I rented a boat. I took my kids, then five, five, and seven, out on the boat—on my own. I think my son sensed my apprehension even though I tried to appear calm and in control. I was afraid! I was afraid I might hit something, or one of the kids would fall out, or I wouldn't be able to start the motor if we stopped, or I'd toss the anchor over and wouldn't be able to get it back up, or I would forget the way back to the dock, and the dock, *oh my goodness how would I dock this boat?*

Even with cloudy skies, wind, and mildly choppy water, I did it. We caught some good sized bass within minutes of anchoring. Beginner's luck, I hit a sweet spot. Success! We all had fun and it felt so good. I rewrote so many stories that day. Stories that once kept me anchored to a belief that I couldn't do things on my own. That day on the boat with my children experiencing the same joy I once did, opened my eyes to a new world. I wasn't going to stop there. The belief of needing someone else to bring my dreams to life was losing traction in my mind. If I could do *this* on my own, why not all the other things I wanted to do?

I am strong. I am brave. I've got this.

Stephen R. Covey said, *"If the ladder is not leaning against the right wall, every step we take just gets us to the wrong place faster."* I finally moved my ladder. I am moving from surviving to exploring. Though just baby steps, new adventures are just around the corner. It is time to do more than survive. It's time to thrive and be happy. I'm not exactly sure what is in store but I know that whatever it is, I will manage just fine. I have a voice. And I will never be silenced again. That little girl who could do anything, she's still here. She's peeking around the corner. She's getting braver and stronger every day. She's got this, and so do you.

CHAPTER NINE

Those Whom You Trust Can
Too Do Great Harm

*"As strong or as tough as people paint me out
to be, I knew I could not do this on my own."*

MLLE ELIZABETH ANN

MLLE ELIZABETH ANN

Elizabeth grew up in a small town in Ontario with big dreams of one day becoming a French teacher. She completed her undergraduate degree at the University of Waterloo in the Honors French Teaching Specialization program, and her Bachelor of Education at Nipissing University. Throughout her undergraduate studies, she lived and studied abroad in both France and Quebec.

The last six years have been more than challenging, one blow after the next. It all started with the sudden and unexpected loss of her mother when Elizabeth was twenty-one, followed by a broken relationship and engagement three months before her wedding, crippling anxiety, and a sexual assault within the first few weeks of a new school year. Elizabeth has had her share of hardships, battles, and obstacles to overcome. Although it has not been easy, she is a true believer in riding out the emotions and confronting them head on: the good, the bad, and the ugly. She finds peace in sharing her story and trying to help those who have suffered similar hardships.

www.mlleelizabethann.ca
ig: @mlle.elizabeth.ann | fb: @elizabeth.ann.author
Photograph: Ben Lariviere Photography

THE INITIAL PAIN

The following are excerpts from my personal journal, written in the weeks that followed my sexual assault.

"This is not an easy decision to make, and it makes me even more vulnerable than I already am. As crazy and as daunting as the process is going to be, I KNOW that I'm making the right decision, BUT it's not that simple. I just feel like the Universe is playing cruel games with me."

The guilt I forced upon myself, the fear of being followed, the agony of not knowing how everything would play out, all left me crippled both physically and mentally. I was ashamed of myself. A part of me felt as if I did this to myself. A week after the assault happened, I told my doctor I just felt like I couldn't do my job anymore. I couldn't leave my apartment. I couldn't do anything. I questioned teaching and whether I actually wanted to do it anymore. Something I had been dreaming of since I was a child and had spent the last six years working toward suddenly seemed insurmountable. Why? All because of one twenty-five-minute appointment with someone I had known for five years and trusted completely.

Sexual assault is a complex and controversial topic that is not easily defined. The Department of Justice (Canada) states that a sexual assault is committed in circumstances of a sexual nature, such that the sexual integrity of the victim is violated.[1] As in my case, the statistics are alarming: sexual assaults perpetrated by someone other than a spouse are least likely to come to the attention

---

1   Canada Department of Justice. 2016. "An Estimation of the Economic Impact of Violent Victimization in Canada, 2009." Accessed July 8, 2019. https://www.justice.gc.ca/eng/rp-pr/cj-jp/victim/rr14_01/p10.html

of police; in fact, ninety percent are *not* reported to police.[2] It is esti-
mated that less than one percent (0.3 percent) of the perpetrators of
sexual assault are held accountable, while over ninety-nine percent
are not. Where is the justice in this?

What I think is important to remember is that one assault does
not *outdo* another. We cannot compare my assault to that of someone else. Assault is assault, plain and simple. The circumstances
leading up to it or the events that transpire after *should not* and
cannot be compared. What I experienced personally is equally as
important, and equally as painful and traumatic, as the experiences
of another. Was I violated? One hundred percent. Did I ask for the
events to unfold as they did? Absolutely not. What upsets me and
rattles me to my core is that the survivor is always ridiculed for
wearing the wrong outfit, or saying the wrong thing at the wrong
time, or giving someone the wrong idea or impression. It seems
we as a society always look for a justification for events, and it is
much easier to come up with a reason why something happened.
*"Well, something they said must have provoked the person to com-
mit the act. She was probably flirting with him so he thought she
was interested in more."* This can't be further from the truth. For
me, someone I trusted enough to share the difficulties and trials of
my life, shattered my trust in those few short moments. I went in for
just another appointment to seek help. It quickly turned into one of
my biggest nightmares.

As hard as it is to define sexual assault or to understand why it
happens, it can be just as hard to get the support we need to overcome such traumatic events. I wrote this chapter to be a voice for
those who have suffered in silence and have been overcome by the
fear, pain, or ramifications for reporting a sexual assault. To those
who have suffered, I'm here to tell you: you are not alone. I'm
here to tell you that while reporting is the hardest decision you will
probably ever have to make, it is the best decision to make. You are
more than a victim: you are a survivor.

Looking back, the best decision I made through this whole process was to call the police that night. I remember that conversation
quite vividly. "I need some advice," I told the female officer, "I had

2   Ontario Ministry of Children. n.d. "Statistics: Sexual Violence." Accessed July 21,
2019. http://www.women.gov.on.ca/owd/english/ending-violence/sexual_violence.shtml

something happen to me and I'm not quite sure what to do about it."After listening without interruption, she assured me that what had happened to me was *not* right. She told me to call back the next day and ask for the Special Victims Unit. In Canada, police services are administered on three different levels: federal, provincial, and municipal.[3] Depending on what province or the city you reside in, the name of the unit or department you seek in reporting assault may be different. Some of the most common examples are the Special Victims Unit, Sex Crimes Unit, or Sexual Assault and Victim Services. This division of my local police force deserves much recognition. In addition to my call, the detective that I worked with had over twenty calls that month alone, whether it be to report a sexual assault, a domestic dispute, child abuse or neglect. My traumatic experience reminded me of the great work our police force plays in the community. She may never read this, but to the detective who helped me through every step of this process, I thank you.

MY JOURNEY

Before I met with the police officer a day and a half after the assault, and before I even told anyone other than a select few individuals, I chose to write. One of the ways I was able to release and process all the emotions I was feeling was through the use of personal journaling. The beauty in journaling is that no one has to know. No one has to read the content you pour onto the pages. You can write it out, rip it up, start again, burn it, whatever speaks to you. There is nothing more cathartic than having a place or an outlet to forget about fear and judgement and just be authentically you. A place where you can say you're afraid, you're hurting, you're in need of help. I spent hours upon hours crying and writing out how I truly felt, sharing some of the details I couldn't bear to share with anyone else but myself. As cliché as it may sound, when we bottle up our emotions, our pain, our insecurities, it is only a matter of time before we find ourselves bursting at the seams.

---

3   Statistics Canada. 2017. "Police resources in Canada, 2016." Accessed July 12, 2019. https://www150.statcan.gc.ca/n1/pub/85-002-x/2017001/article/14777-eng.htm

I knew, however, that journaling wouldn't be the only solution, or the only tool I would need to overcome the battle I faced. This is why I'm a firm believer that there is absolutely no shame in seeking professional help.

After giving my formal video statement to the police, I was immediately given a resource for free counseling provided through my local Sexual Assault and Domestic Violence Treatment Centre. As a single woman with bills to pay, having the option for free counseling was a life saver. My counselor was trained and had experience with trauma often rooting from sexual assault. She helped me through six of the hardest months of my life. It is so easy to get lost in our thoughts and negative feelings that we forget to put things in perspective. As strong or as tough as people paint me out to be, I knew I could not do this on my own. I didn't know how to process what happened or to understand the brain's response to trauma. I've dealt with death and a relationship crumbling, but had never experienced being a victim, being violated in a very personal way. Was it normal to feel guilt? Was it normal to blame myself? These were some of the tough questions I had to work through with my counselor.

ANSWERING THE TOUGH QUESTIONS

The answer is yes. Yes, it's only human to feel guilt, like you brought this upon yourself. Yes, it's normal to blame ourselves because there is obviously something we did to cause the problem. Wrong! But this is the problem with assault. We as a society have for some unknown and unexplainable reason put the blame on the survivor. In the court system, it's the same. During a trial, the survivor has to take the stand and testify. The survivor gets questioned and gets torn apart by the defence lawyers, while the perpetrator gets to sit back and watch the whole process unravel in front of them. The perpetrator is not always held accountable for their alleged actions, but the survivor is forced to relive the experience and be on the defensive about every single decision they made leading up to, during, or after the assault.

It is not easy trying to live with the pain and uncertainty that lies ahead after a sexual assault. The constant replaying of everything that happened in your mind. But this is where my journal has been my saving grace because if I ever doubted myself, I know I have everything written down exactly how it happened. And my journaling continues. Every night before I go to bed, I write down the things that I'm grateful for. Trying to change our mindset from suffering and pain, to being grateful goes a long way. Shortly after the assault happened, I remember writing, *"Today I'm grateful I made it through the day."* It may seem so trivial, but it was the truth. By owning and accepting our feelings, no matter how hard or how painful they are to express, over time, gratitude will help to make those struggles we're facing a little more bearable. We take back the power that society has tried to strip from us, and we show the world that we are *not* to be blamed.

SPEAK UP. END THE STIGMA.

According to the World Health Organization (WHO), the reasons women do not report sexual violence include: inadequate support systems; shame; fear or risk of retaliation; fear or risk of being blamed; fear or risk of not being believed; fear or risk of being mistreated or socially ostracized.[4] As I mentioned, the hardest obstacle to overcome for me personally was the feeling of being ashamed of myself. In my journal I wrote, *"I did this to myself."* As I thought about the future and how this may all unfold in court, I experienced the fear of being socially ostracized. I immediately thought everyone would paint me as the slut looking for attention, as there is a background story of social media use and exchanges via Snapchat. With help from my counselor and close family, though, I was reminded that this person preyed on my vulnerability, as he knew everything about me and my life. All of a sudden that fear then turned to guilt. Guilt of coming forward and how it could ruin his life, his career. Who cared what it did to *me*? I am ruining *him*. The female police officer who took my original call reminded me, "The bottom line is what he did was *wrong*, and he broke every level of

---

4   World Health Organization. 2012. "Understanding and addressing violence against women." Accessed July 12, 2019 https://apps.who.int/iris/bitstream/handle/10665/77434/WHO_RHR_12.37_eng.pdf;jsessionid=2A2676C0085957BED206B15F29CD1767?sequence=1

professionalism given his job in alternative medicine." As the old saying goes, he made his bed, now he has to lie in it.

As I look back and reflect on what happened, and with my trial coming up in the near future, there is one very important message that keeps replaying in my mind, and that I wish to leave as a reminder to us all. It is most often the people whom we trust that can do so much harm in the span of just a few minutes. Think about that for a second. Those we trust can harm us. I don't share this to make you question every person or every relationship that you have in your life, but the statistics are overwhelming. According to SACHA Sexual Assault Centre, the perpetrator is known to the victim in eighty-two percent of sexual assaults.[5] Drugs, alcohol, flirting, walking home alone at night are *not* the cause of sexual assaults: it is the perpetrator.

Regardless of the pain this traumatic experience caused, and still causes me, I always try to face the reality of the situation. In a survey, fifty-three percent of survivors responded that they did not report their sexual assault because they were not confident in the police. Two out of three—yes you read that right, *two* out of *three*— survivors responded that they were not confident in the criminal justice and court system, and therefore decided to let the assault "disappear," like it never happened.[6] I'm proud to say I decided to be that one out of three to stand up and bring awareness to the harsh realities victims face on a daily basis. Because of my decision to come forward and report my sexual assault to the police, more people came forward after me. If a perpetrator has gotten away with it once, why wouldn't they try again? As hard a decision as reporting was to make, I wanted to stop this from happening again. At one pivotal moment, I made the conscious decision to put my fear of the unknown aside in the hope of making a difference for those who suffer in silence.

* * *

As I prepare for trial, I re-read my journal and try to anticipate the road ahead. I question myself, fall into the trap of self-doubt and fear of repercussion, and question whether I'm making everything

---

5   SACHA. n.d. "Statistics." Accessed July 15, 2019. http://sacha.ca/resources/statistics

6   See note 5 above.

up. Regardless of the backlash I may face and the unknown that haunts me, I know deep down in my soul that I'm telling the truth. Every. Single. Part. I'm confident in the reality that deep down, I know I made the right call. Although it was probably the hardest decision I have ever made, it was a decision I had to make on my own and on my own terms. A lot of my immediate future is uncertain, but one thing I do know is I *refuse* to let another ninety-nine percent of perpetrators get away with the pain they inflict by the unforgiving acts that happen on a daily basis. We need to send a clear message that we are strong, that we support each other, and that what is happening in the world around us needs to change. If you're a victim: be brave and don't be afraid. If you love someone who has been violated: listen, comfort, and offer your support. The world is a better place when we love each other.

* * *

All of the emotions and all of the information we must process when reporting sexual assault can be undeniably overwhelming. I understand that coming forward is not always that easy or that simple. I was fortunate to receive many resources after going to the police, but this is not always the case. Some women are left alone to live with the guilt and the shame, and they simply don't know what to do with what happened. If you can identify with any of these feelings or circumstances, here is some help that I hope will guide you to make the decisions you need to make.

The Victim Services Directory (VSD) was created by the Policy Centre for Victim Issues of the Department of Justice Canada, to help victims and individuals locate services for crimes committed across Canada.[7] On the right-hand side of the website, you can begin a search for Victim Services by entering a postal code to pick your location within a specific kilometer range. The next screen allows you to customize your search with filters for specifications such as types of victimization (abuse, assault, homicide, etc.) and types of services provided (counseling, shelters or transition homes, support groups, etc.); for an even more detailed search, you can specify which gender you identify with or what language of communica-

---

7   Canada Department of Justice. 2015. "Victim Services Directory." Accessed July 15, 2019. https://www.justice.gc.ca/eng/cj-jp/victims-victimes/vsd-rsv/index.html

tion you prefer, all to get the most accurate and accommodating services possible. After having gone through this experience as your average twenty-seven-year-old woman, my advice is that if something happens to you and you have the slightest shred of feeling that it was wrong or inappropriate, the police should always be the first phone call you make. If they do not offer any supplementary support in the process, I hope this website will be a second step in the right direction for you to get the help you deserve.

LIFE MUST GO ON.

It's been near two years since my assault and I'm still anxiously awaiting the days of my trial. I'll be honest—some days are easier than others. My circumstances of life are different than most my age, as not many lose their mother in their 20s. Why do I mention this? Because although she can't be with me here in the physical world, she is my driving force that pushes me forward, on my darkest of days. On the days I can't comprehend how I function or make it through, I think of her and know she is my reason.

So if you can promise me one thing, it is that you find that "someone" or "something" that gives you the motivation and the strength to be the strong survivor you are. We must not let the actions of someone else cripple and destroy our lives that we've worked so hard to build. Movement is being made, slowly but surely in the justice system. I know this all too well. This progress however, will not continue to be successful if we hide in the shadow of our uncertainties and fears of the unknown road that lies ahead. I chose to no longer be silent. We *MUST* no longer be silent. Life does go on, I'll agree, but how it goes on is dependent on how you choose to make it happen. Be strong. Stand up. Please, be silent no more.

CHAPTER TEN

History Repeating

"Each day I struggle with my brain, my heart, and my intuition, but it has never steered me wrong."

SASHA ROSE

Sasha Rose is a woman with big ideas and dreams. She learned from her mother and two sisters that when you have an idea, you put it into action and see it through. Sasha is a budding entrepreneur, with her most recent venture being Oneida Bistro (located South of Ottawa, ON).

Sasha has always wanted to be a mother, and has now been gifted with the ever challenging and rewarding title of mama to her two daughters. She hopes to find a way to make a small difference in this world for her girls to grow up safe and confident.

Sasha is a spiritual woman and an avid animal and outdoor lover. She strives for the life she has always wanted; to own a hobby farm with her family. Sasha is currently working toward her 200-hour yoga teacher certification to heal herself and others. Sasha comes from a mixed background including Scottish, English, and French-Canadian on her mother's side, and Chinese and First Nations-Canadian on her father's side.

ig: @sasharose_4 | @theroseregrowth
fb: @sasharose4

My memories often reflect on a time when I was young and the world was peaceful. I grew up with my two sisters, mother, father, and all the chaos of visitors that came with our family's open-door policy. We bounced around from home to home with our pets; one house with an above ground pool, a house with a vegetable garden and weeping willow tree, and also a teeny-tiny house on ten acres. Moving was our norm—a new house every year or two meant new areas to explore.

I was a happy child with an immense imagination for creating scenes out of my thousands of toys alongside my sisters. My mother was, and still is, the caregiver; I can still taste the stews and casseroles she created for the entire family—without complaint. She cared for us entirely—without complaint. She also ran a business from home, all while tending to the hoards of kids, and puppy after puppy. She kept the ship sailing—without complaint.

I loved my parents, but was a complete daddy's girl. When I was ill, I would try to crawl into his bed, despite his horrendous snoring, only to be kicked out because he was intoxicated. I constantly waited at his shop door to smell the fresh cut sawdust. As I got older, it was harder to gain access to his shop. I wanted to spend any chance I could with my father, maybe because the time spent together was exciting; ferry rides to Grandma's house, amusement parks, ice cream and mini donuts. I took my mother for granted as a child; she wasn't going anywhere, she was solid, she was consistent, she was safe. I never appreciated all that she did until I became a mother.

My father wasn't around at many milestones or events: dog agility competitions, horseback riding lessons, birthday parties, or camping trips. My mother was. He began to get easily agitated; when I was seven, I remember being crouched against my maroon bedroom wall with horse wallpaper, while he yelled closely in my face . . . *what had I done to make him so angry?* This behavior changed my admiration for him; my love began to fade; he began to unravel.

When I was eight, my life turned upside down, this is how I remember the day my family fell apart. Explosive, muffled yelling emerged from my mother's bedroom, it sounded like my father threw my mother against the door. She was trying to keep him from releasing his anger on the household and wreaking havoc in front of us. My oldest sister, only about twelve years old, demanded that our father leave. She made sure our other sister and I were out of harm's way by getting us to stay in our bedroom—that same one with maroon walls. Our father distanced himself from us and was always sad, full of guilt, so pitiful, with tears in his eyes and beer on his breath. *Why did he not want to be near me? Why did I make him sad? Why won't my mom let us see him?*

When I was eleven I was living in a small town with my sisters and my mother; we were living in rental number four or five since our father left. My mother continued to work incredibly hard to keep a roof over our heads, clothing on our backs, and food in our bellies, with zero help from our father. He called on and off, sent birthday cards, and visited us once. He made promises to call me every day, but that never came true.

The final time speaking with my father was around my twelfth birthday—I was sick with the flu and a high fever—I swiftly told him to "fuck off," he shattered every promise ever made and I was heart broken. Now that I was a bit older to understand what was happening to him, the addiction and abuse, and the lies began to surface, I cut that tie and never looked back.

My father was my idol, my hero, my dad. In true "Hanson" woman fashion, I brushed off my heartbreak only to have it resurface two decades later. I never realized how much resentment I had toward my father and how it impacted my adult life, and now my children.

* * *

Fresh out of a long-term relationship, I reconnected with an old acquaintance; he paid attention to me, was eager to meet up, and expressed he had a crush on me since high school. What was the harm, right? He was a different type of guy; goofy, tried hard to make me laugh, affectionate, had long-term friends, and a stable job. We spent time together and rushed into a relationship—this is where the trouble began.

> *Has the hair on the back of your neck ever stood*
> *up, just by the way someone looks at you?*

He soon became controlling and antisocial; I am not a partier, but I did enjoy drinking with a close-knit group of friends. He began to shut down, as if he was asleep with his eyes open, with an angered look on his face. I remember my best friend asking me, "does he hate me?" Of course I defended him and said "no, he must just be tired."

He was a messy homebody and I had little patience for his laziness. So, after our first official argument about six months into dating, *Mr. Hyde* emerged out of the blue and I felt like he had taken off a mask. His goofy façade vanished and there was this pent up being standing before me; his back slightly arched, but still managing to stand tall, his head tilted to the side in the attempt to avoid eye contact. My defence wall went sky high. He began to pace in front of the door and would not let me leave our room; speaking in a lowered, yet firm voice; he talked at me, not to me. He started to stand up straighter with each word and slowly moved closer to me. The alarm bells were ringing in my head and my heart began to race. His demeaning behavior was not taken lightly and I kicked him out immediately. I had never experienced that fear before; sheer anger, an insane heart rate, and a flu like fever rushed over me.

He proceeded to follow me for weeks; I'd come home to him on my doorstep, staring silently, leaving cigarette butts all over the deck. He would try to come into my house, I stood my ground and refused—I could tell this made his blood boil. He would send me text messages, "why are you wearing my favorite shirt? You're a tease," as my friend and I walked through town. I ignored these messages and went on with my life and he finally just went away, or so I thought.

I became good at being the solo pilot in my life. My friend and I found another rental in town and I quickly learned that my crazy ex lived down the road. He had a girlfriend, so we texted occasionally. I enjoyed being with my friends, hosting dinner parties (with drinks), and having games nights (with drinks). I made the bad decision of inviting *you know who* and his friends over for a small party. He insisted that he broke up with his girlfriend, and that he wasn't happy; she was too clingy, *blah, blah, blah.* I believed him. It wasn't until years later that I found out he had been cheating on her for quite some time with me. History repeated.

Fast forward six weeks and my period was a week late—*fuck.* I had to tell him and he said "you're fucking kidding, right?" and then a switch flipped and he said, "I've always loved you." The mixed emotions in his words confused me, we weren't even together. He quickly moved in to "care" for me, and we stayed together because I was pregnant. I cannot say this enough, just because you find yourself unexpectedly expecting, doesn't mean you need to stay with him. I wish I took my own advice.

His old behavior returned instantly, but I felt stuck. I sadly had an early miscarriage; I had accepted my growing peanut and was excited to be a mama. We stayed together because I didn't want the judgement of "she was only with him because she got knocked up."

In an effort to stay positive, we made plans to move for a fresh start. I felt light and motivated for a new adventure! I got a job and had plans to attend university. He sat on his ass collecting unemployment, drinking beer in the yard, and "searching" for work.

Two months after moving, I was pregnant again; I was thrilled. I'm not sure how to express the utter disappointment and resentment in his voice when he said "now I have to tell my parents *you're* pregnant again." The news was not well received. He became closed off again and had a short fuse, he'd detach and sit in the yard for hours. I put the pressure on him to find work, anything to help our growing family. His solution, out of province work; he got a full-time job and insisted that we move. I was adamant on staying close to my mother, this was my first child! He visited once a month and I went through pregnancy alone. I learned to be content with my two dogs and my growing belly. I developed some health issues and decided it was time for him to come home, help me, and get serious about putting down some roots. He refused. I felt panicked and scared to be alone. My mother suggested I move into her small cabin, back in my little home town. I accepted. *Why didn't I leave him then?*

After giving birth, things got even worse. Maybe it was post-partum depression, or maybe I just had a crappy partner.

Have you ever felt terribly alone, even while
your partner is right beside you?

Months passed without speaking, unless it was him asking what's for dinner. I felt isolated, my only communication was with my mother, the rare visitor, and goo-goo-gah-gah with my baby. He took one week off and began sleeping in the other room—he needed his rest—que my blood boiling resentment for him. I broke down in tears once when my daughter was being fussy (frustration and lack of sleep got the better of me), and he laughed at me. He said I was stupid for getting upset, that I needed to calm down.

Mr. Hyde reappeared one day while he was giving our daughter a bottle, he was in such a hurry for her to take a nap; she dozed on and off until he became so frustrated that he got up abruptly from the couch and threw her bottle across the room, hitting a picture on the wall. I yelled for him to give me the baby. He (not so cautiously) passed me our daughter and stormed out. My heart raced, tears welled in my eyes, and my daughter cried. *How was I to feel comfortable leaving her alone with him?*

Have you ever felt trapped in your own body
or your own home? Like you are on auto-pilot,
doing your mundane day-to-day tasks without
even realizing?

I was a single mother with a "man," an incapable adult, living in my home. I cooked and cleaned for him, cared for his child, and eventually went back to work full-time. He would return from work, remove his diesel soaked coveralls, and leave them on the kitchen floor. We'd eat dinner, he'd then lay on the floor with our daughter for thirty minutes, then head to the shower for an hour, minimum. After, he would sink into the couch, beer in hand, and get lost in his phone—the blue hue would light his face as I snuggled our baby to sleep. I kept the ship sailing—without complaint.

He put me down constantly. Putting on clean clothes was met with, "who are you getting dolled up for?" His feelings about me having a home-based business, "if you put as much effort into the house and our kid as you do in your work, things would be better." He would sarcastically and disgustedly say, "at least I shower for you." I had become an empty shell, a slave to him and his expectations. I forced a smile, hid my tears, and attempted conversations with him. He could not read my body language, he ignored my sadness, he forced himself upon me, and my biggest fear was becoming pregnant again. I knew I needed out.

Does your partner hide your arguments and
behave differently with you in private?

Everything happened behind closed doors, or he'd insist on going for a drive. He'd make me ask my mom to babysit or he'd wait until it was late at night (knowing I wouldn't cause a scene). I obeyed to appease him, I didn't want to be *difficult.*

His ability to consume the room was daunting. One day, we sat in the living room full of tension; as if we were playing a game of chicken, who would lash out first? He thought he was safe to *express himself*; his voice became loud with jumbled words, his gaze rose to reach mine. I trembled inside, but tried to appear calm. I begged him to please relax, our daughter was in the room. He stood up and began to pace, my heart began thumping faster. I asked for him to sit down—he ignored me. I leaned toward him to try to get his attention, asking him to calm down—he ignored me. I stood up and yelled back, "enough! can I speak?" He laughed in my face. As he yelled, my mother and sister came home. My mom saw me cradling my child tightly as I rushed down the hallway away from him, she stormed toward him with thunder clouds in her eyes. "Don't hurt him," I cried out with tears streaming down my face. *Why the hell was I protecting him?*

He was abusive; psychologically and verbally, and he lashed out at my dogs. He once grabbed my one dog from the kennel by his collar, lifted him off the ground, and threw him while yelling at me. On another occasion, our newly adopted puppy had an accident while we stayed in a hotel. As she squatted to pee, he kicked her in the hip, knocking her over, and she screamed in pain. She required surgery we couldn't afford and still limps to this day.

I needed distance and my sister gave me the opportunity to visit her in Toronto with my daughter; I used this week away to clear the cobwebs from my brain, I barely spoke to him. We arrived home the last week of June. I carried Jayden and our bags past him, barely saying a word. "That wasn't the hello I was expecting," he said, disappointed that I clearly had not been missing him. June 30 that year was the end. I told him that for Canada Day I would be going to the parade with our daughter and he was not welcome to join us. I was done.

We sat in my living room, surprisingly calm after the split, and I said "imagine if our girl came home and said the person she is dating treats her the way you treat me, how would you feel?" He stared at me and it clicked. All he had to say was, "no one will replace me as her dad." People don't put words like that into the universe unless they believe the opposite may happen, it's like someone saying "I'll never hurt you, I'll never cheat on you." I never let our relationship escalate to a physical explosion like that of my mother and father because my intuition screamed at me to get out.

Get out while you can.

To this day, he still maintains some level of control over my life; co-parenting is hard. Over the years my life has advanced; relocating to a new town, having a second daughter, moving houses, having our daughter full-time, then part-time, then full-time again, getting married, and most-recently, a lengthy court battle to be granted permission to move my family to Ontario. Each time I reach a new level of "adulthood," he tries to force his way back into my life, using our daughter as a pawn.

I see my father's behaviors in him and realize a piece of my childhood was repeating itself, now for my daughter. The grand gestures; meals out, fun toys, hotel stays, movies all the time, and long drives to new places. However, these started to fade as his bank account shrunk. Eventually, the visits became distant, so did the phone calls, and the time together wasn't as joyful. The worst though, making promises he can't keep, "I'll call you every day, I'll see you every weekend."

I have learned to set boundaries and speak up when things weren't in her best interest. I understand that caving and giving into your abuser is much, much easier than standing up, but that only gives them more power—do not give them that satisfaction. I have shed buckets of tears on my daughter's behalf and do my best to protect her from the damage that abandonment from a father can do. Each day I struggle with my brain, my heart, and my intuition, but it has never steered me wrong. The battles brought on by trusting myself have been hard, but they forced me to be a tougher, more compassionate version of myself.

My father wanted nothing to do with us once my mother moved us to a new town; this day may also come for my girl. If it does, I am confident she will be picked back up by a badass group of women. Myself, her aunties, and her Nana have all dealt with abandonment and we can handle it.

* * *

If you find yourself feeling lost within yourself, your home, or your life, look around you. What is triggering your rapid heart rate? Your sweaty palms and anxiety? What are your dreams telling you to confront? It will be uncomfortable, you will cry, but you will heal. Speak up to a friend, a family member, a therapist, or even an acquaintance; sometimes speaking to someone at a distance can be the most therapeutic. Sit with yourself and your conscience and do what is right for you.

STRONGER THAN YOU THINK

Amber Phillips

I was disappointed in myself when I realized what was happening. The subtle insults. The control he held over my life.

I was mad at myself for letting it happen. Why did I let it continue for years?

I was pissed off at the world for not seeing that I needed help. Why didn't I ask for help?

I felt alone, thinking no one would believe me. Why would they? He fooled me into believing there was only him.

But most of all, I felt weak; I deserved it, I wasn't good enough. He closed my eyes to the world, he held me down.

But I am good enough; I didn't deserve it. It just took me being nudged by my best friend to listen to the voice in my head, to take a hard look inside my little world to see it.

I am not weak, and neither are you .

I woke up. I chose to live. I began my life.

He buried me within his world, little did he know, he had planted a seed that would soon outgrow him.

No one deserves to be abused. No one "has it coming."

Realizing that you need help is half the battle. Understanding that the situation is not your fault is the other half.

You are not weak for not realizing what was happening sooner. You are not weak for not seeing the red flags.

You have an internal strength that you may not even realize is within. A strength to take back control and to walk away from your abuser.

It takes strength to rebuild your life after living in hell. It takes strength to move forward and heal.

It also takes time. Healing will not happen overnight. It can take months, or even years. Some days it'll feel like one step forward and two steps back. But you will heal.

Be proud of your scars, for they show that you are a survivor and a warrior.

You are stronger than you give yourself credit for. Never let anyone tell you otherwise.

SECTION THREE

Be You, Bravely: Let Go of the Shit That
Suffocates Your Soul

*"She was powerful, not because she wasn't
scared but because she went on so strongly,
despite the fear."* -ATTICUS

FEATURING

Beth Driscoll
Angel Kibble
Stephanie Reid
Kady Romagnuolo
Mandy Karpoff
Kiki Carr
Whitney Stout
Eldyka Simpson

You often feel tired,
not because you've done too
much, but because you've
done too little of what sparks
a light in you.

HER VOICE

Beth Driscoll

The last few years, there have been monumental changes in my life as I continue to let go of the things that no longer serve me.

Among those changes was a decision made about a year ago to switch to an alcohol free lifestyle. It was a long awaited decision, as my inner voice gradually rose from a whisper to a shout—repeating the same message over and over again—it was the one thing holding me back from living up to my potential.

As an introvert—a deeply private person at my core—I hesitated sharing this. I've been dancing with vulnerability and transparency for years, and have been inspired to speak my truth by those brave enough to share their own stories.

As the months in recovery bridge the gap between where I once was to where I am now, I can now reflect with clarity on some of the elements it took to get me here.

An essential word that has helped me through this process is "choice". Behind any major habit change, has to be a mindset shift first. Choices in terms of day-to-day life, and the small choices that have a big, everlasting effect. I have a choice as to which thoughts I will allow to permeate in my mind, or release; I have a choice in the people I share my energy and time with; I have a choice in whether to isolate myself or reach out to others; I have a choice, not in what happens to me, but how I react to it.

Another essential part of my journey has been the realization that humans need each other. My substance abuse was a great hiding place. When I realized I needed to make a change, I clung so tightly to my independence, that it took great time for me to reach out to others. I clearly remember feeling the distinct and utter terror moving my feet towards the first few group meetings I attended. I was fighting gravity every step of the way, but something inside kept moving forward. Connection is the antidote to addiction. The phrase is familiar to me now, but sometimes it takes stepping into a space with strangers that share the same experiences to finally be understood.

We have all heard the saying "It takes a village to raise a child." Hell, I think it takes a village to RAISE UP an ADULT. Humans are wired for connection. We all need to know that others can relate to us, that we matter, that we are worthy: And sometimes we need to hear it from others until we can say it for ourselves.

I am sharing my truth for this very reason; in case someone out there needs to hear this:

It's *okay* to make a different choice.

It's *okay* to question the role of things in your life. It's ok to question how certain things play a role in your life.

It's *okay* to let those things go; whether it be a person, a substance, a habit, a job, society's or someone else's expectations, a mindset, or a belief.

While I have been letting things go, I have also been finding things, such as my authenticity and my voice. These have always been there, waiting for me to discover them and make them useful.

For me, the pivotal clarity at the end of this is that we are limited, but only by our own beliefs;

we do recover;

we do find our voice;

we then use them for a greater good.

"Our deepest fear is not that we are inadequate. Our deepest fear is that we are powerful beyond measure. It is our light, not our darkness that most frightens us."
                                        -Marianne Williamson

CHAPTER ELEVEN

Rise Above the Ashes

"I am not defined by my past; it empowers me to live a purpose driven life"

ANGEL KIBBLE

Angel Kibble is a mother, author, and Canadian Army Veteran who opens up about her life's journey hoping to empower those living with chronic pain and mental health issues surrounding abuse and injustice.

After having been forced to medically release from the Canadian Armed Forces, she was left living with numerous diagnoses including Complex Regional Pain Syndrome and Post Traumatic Stress Disorder. Despite others trying to keep her as the *victim,* she has survived by relying on her inner strength, determination, resilience, and focusing on the well-being of herself and her children. She uses her passion for writing to share her incredible journey from trauma to healing and rebuilding. Angel is a newly rising author and Trauma Informed Certified Coach working towards certification in Mindfulness Based Stress Reduction and Yoga Therapy. She embraces a holistic approach to the challenges of life while maintaining a slower pace and allowing a healthy balance between living with disabilities and nurturing her soul. Born in Sarnia, Ontario, and spending most of her youth in the Okanagan, Angel now resides with her husband, children, and her service dog on beautiful Vancouver Island. Her journey through life, though not as she envisioned, is one of hope, inspiration, and true resilience. Being the warrior she is, Angel will continue to share stories from her soul in future publications including an upcoming book series.

www.AngelEmpowerment.ca
ig: @AngelEmpowerment | fb: @AngelEmpowerment
p: @AngelEmpowerment
goodreads: Angel Empowerment

I was silenced through most of my life despite my *inner voice*, which has always screamed my truths. I silenced *her* many times as I chose the road of less contention, yet time after time I felt confused, shamed, powerless, alone, and completely defeated. The more I educated myself, the more I saw how interconnected a lifetime of abuse and dysfunction was and the heavy toll it had taken on me. How do I tell you about such a lifetime in a single chapter? I simply cannot. I have experienced much adversity in my life and could easily describe a single situation where I was silenced and how I found my voice to give you something you may relate to, the tools needed to take action, and how to make change in your own life; however, there isn't just one thing—rather a lifetime of events—that has brought me to who and where I am today. The best "tools" I found were my inner voice, my intuition, and trusting my survival instincts. Breaking the silence that once ruled me was the beginning of my lengthy, soul wrenching, healing journey. Life's experiences are much like a painting where each stroke interconnects, blends, and is layered with mistakes, corrections, and fluidity to create a final product. Like art, we are never perfect, however unlike art, we are always in a state of developing, growing, and evolving. Seeing the true beauty in something or someone requires us to look deeper so we can appreciate the pain, agony, and struggles that came before. Anyone and anything can present well and although no one can ever know the truths of another's journey, we can share our stories and gain unimaginable strength in voicing them.

I grew up hearing traumatic stories about my conception, my mother's pregnancy, and my first few years of life. If my mother had never shared these horrific stories with me, I never would have felt my life started so traumatically. She had married young, as many did in the sixties, and in a span of thirteen months, she and her husband welcomed a baby girl followed by a boy; my older siblings. A few years later for reasons only she knows, my mother left her husband, their family home, and moved in with her husband's co-worker who went on to become my biological father. When my mother shared stories about my father and I, she referred to me as "the monster that grew inside"; words no child should ever hear. These stories naturally created deep painful wounds on my soul. Unknowingly, I was born into multigenerational layers of dysfunction, abuse and unmanaged mental health issues that would take me a lifetime to sort through the ashes, break free, rise above and rebuild from. The early years of my life continued with chaos and uncertainty. My parents separated shortly after my conception while my mother hid my existence from my father. I was placed with my mother's brother for a few months. Poverty, dysfunction, upheaval and abuse paved the way during my formative years. My parents reconciled when I was six months old; when my father finally learned of me, his beautiful daughter with big blue eyes and the blondest hair, just like him. Reconciliation, however, was short-lived. At barely two years old my mother packed our belongings, myself, and my siblings into our pickup truck. We drove through the dark cascades of the Rocky Mountains as we headed west while my father unknowingly slept. Settling into a new life, my mother met a kind man who soon became my stepfather. My mother, my siblings (six and seven years older), and I moved in with him and I proudly named him, "daddy." My first memories begin here. Daddy, along with his sisters and their families, owned and operated a large pig farm in a most picturesque setting amongst the mountains, farm fields, forests and a crystal clear river. There were so many new and exciting things, and I was an inquisitive shadow who loved going to work with my daddy. I smile fondly as I recall running around in my rubber boots helping feed and water the sows, mucking out the stalls, riding tractors, smiling at my daddy's rainbow umbrella hat, which protected him from the blistering Okanagan sun, and the distinct strong aroma of freshly cut firewood. I remember our long dirt driveway which was littered with potholes and the distinct sound of the raspy air-cooled Volkswagen engine. Work and social time were surrounded by back breaking labor and time with our new extended family. I didn't know it then, but I believe I was surrounded with love and support that would get me through what lay ahead. The financial devastation of the recession in the eighties saw interest rates skyrocket and many lose their homes, including our farm which was repossessed. We packed up our truck to move on yet again. I watched in disbelief with my nose squished against the window which fogged over from my rapid, shallow breath. The warm tears that silently rolled down my petite cheeks blurred my view of what seemed like a slow motion movie which I had front row tickets for. The unsettling heaviness in my gut was one I would come to know again and again. Intuitively *she* was screaming trying to be heard as *she* knew that leaving the farm would come at a price. Unsure of anything that once was or of what was to come, we drove one last time down our long driveway turning onto the main road. Moments later we rounded the bend and in that instant, the only home I knew was gone. I was left blurry eyed with an incredible heaviness in the pit of my stomach and felt frozen in my own body.

Within an hour our rental truck rolled onto the driveway of the fourplex that was to be our new home. I took a little comfort from the nearby creek as it reminded me of the river at our farm. Daddy and I enjoyed walks together exploring the new neighborhood; the summer breeze teased our senses with the strong aroma of the numerous fruit trees and the gentle hint of fresh chamomile that grew freely like wildflowers. Every walk was a new adventure, and I was happiest by my daddy's side. Despite our new family, dysfunction, abuse, mental health issues, and neglect grew and became the norm of my childhood. I soon became a victim; the product of a dark environment. I longed for connection with my mother and craved her attention however a wedge I could not understand began to separate us more with each passing day. I'm sure more often than I can remember, she was warm, fun, and loving yet my memories are few. Throughout my life she would give the shirt off her back, helping anyone in need and then without warning a switch would flip, and she would be raging, yelling, screaming, and on a rampage. The explosions would come on instantly and without logic. We all walked on eggshells around her as we tried to avoid setting her off. She was as unpredictable and emotionally damaging as a tornado. I never knew where, when, why, or for how long, nor how much devastation she would leave in her path. Whatever her demons, the highs and lows that were my daily existence were like something one would only see in movies. This took a huge toll on many including myself, yet I continued to have front row seats to *movies* that I wish

I never saw. Statistically, I would be set up to repeat the same dysfunctional cycle, which I sadly did for many years.

I fell victim to incest at the hands of my brother, who pregroomed me for predators that followed. He subjected me to ongoing sexual, physical, financial, and emotional abuse. He introduced, provided, and encouraged me to smoke, use drugs, and drink alcohol starting at age nine. My life was filled with uncertainty and I quickly lost all sense of safety. One day after returning from school, I was coldly told by my mother that, "Daddy moved out." At first, I was not even told where he was and over the years I never really knew if they were together or apart. I did know the sense of security and safety that daddy provided was suddenly and painfully stripped away. Without him, the layers of abuse and dysfunction grew each day. Over the years, I did see him on occasion and I looked forward to our annual trips to Alberta to visit his side of the family. I cherished that time with daddy and our large extended Dutch family. There we were free to be the family I always dreamed and prayed for—loving, warm, safe, and I was able to just be a kid. As each visit came to a teary end, we would kiss and hug our family goodbye, taking a deep breath with each hug hoping to remember their scent as it was that of home in my heart. Again, I found myself sitting in the car with my nose squished against the window watching as the city and their loving smiles faded in the distance. The heaviness in the pit of my gut screaming out to me each time as *she* knew the bad things lay ahead once I returned home with my mother. I remained painfully silent, trying to hide every emotion and I got used to putting on a smile and pretending everything was okay. I knew in my gut, through it all, there was more to life than what I could see. I saw glimpses of functional, loving families and I knew there was greater meaning and purpose. Life could be beautiful and I would stop at nothing to be a part of it. I had no idea how or what that would look like, but as a young teen I chose to do whatever it took to break the cycle in which I was conceived and forced to live in. I'd learn how to thrive, rather than just survive.

My journey was not an easy one. I was trying to make sense of stuff that made no sense. I loved going to friends' houses. I dreamed and prayed to God that I could have what others had, ranging from basic needs to extravagant material items, but mostly for a safe family. Initially my friends enjoyed coming to my house as there were no rules and we had complete freedom to do as we pleased, however my brother and his friends reveled in the lack of supervision. One by one my friends stopped coming over and they distanced themselves from me as they too were targeted and victimized by my brother and his friends. My suffering surfaced as a tough outer shell which no one could break, yet the truth was, I was a devastatingly fragile little girl who was desperately trying to survive and escape further abuse. Soon after my daddy moved out again, I came home from school to find we had been evicted and that my mom had left without me. One can only imagine the complete state of shock I was in having been abandoned. Looking back, it was no surprise as our home was a revolving door and flop house for many of my brother's *friends* and *random men*; most days saw a handful of troubled young men crashing at our home with free access to abuse myself and my young friends, forever affecting innocent young impressionable girls. There I was, thirteen years old, standing in the street not knowing where my mother was, where to go or even what to do. Grief disguised herself heavily as anger and agonizing pain from every wrong I had ever been subjected to. It was more than I could bear. Crying and shaking uncontrollably, craving a loving safe home, and having nothing but the clothes on my back, I walked to the highway. With my thumb out it only took moments to catch a ride to the neighboring small town. I stayed with *friends* I met just prior who happily supplied me with all I needed to drown my pain. Eventually I found my mother at the local transition house. We moved into one run down sketchy motel after another. Despite our address changing many times, my unimaginable daily existence didn't. Life only became worse and my tough outer shell thickened. I was labeled a troublemaker and expelled from high school shortly after grade eight began. I desperately wanted someone to love me, believe in me, encourage me, educate and teach me while keeping me safe so I could thrive; instead I lived in constant chaos which worsened over time. After being expelled from school, I spent my time hanging around with other "misfits", most of whom were older men who had their own reasons for spending time with me. I found myself in numerous dangerous situations—yet having never known a different life—I accepted abuse and dysfunction as the norm. I quickly learned that it was easier and less painful in the moment to just give myself to men rather than them taking what they wanted from me when they wanted it. I continued on an extremely destructive course finding myself in the foster and judicial systems where I initially felt comfort in their *structure* and *safety.* Yet I was again targeted by predators within the systems which left me desperately acting out and crying for help. I was angry. I had had enough! The courts assigned a youth worker to help me and surprisingly I became quite attached and quickly grew to trust her. She believed in me and supported me like no one had before. She helped me see I was capable of breaking cycles and that I could be and do anything if I set my mind to it. With her assistance I found and briefly met my biological father in Ontario. My heart longed for a normal life and I prayed to find it with him. Despite my hopes, the universe clearly had other plans. At fifteen and having lived through more than a lifetime of trauma and having no options in sight, I packed the few personal belongings I had, boarded a coach bus and I went to live with a friend and her family on Vancouver Island. Leaving behind everyone and everything that I knew. Wanting more than anything to have a fresh start and despite moving to Vancouver Island on my own at the age of fifteen, I enrolled in high school knowing that an education was key to a positive future. I quickly made friends and started settling into my new environment as best as I could. A few months later, my parents came to visit seeking reconciliation and proposing to move to a nearby neighborhood where we could be the family that I desperately wanted. Like many times before, it started well and then quickly spiralled out of control. The conflict between my mother's instability and my desire to thrive rather than just survive was explosive. I wasn't willing to be abused anymore. The combination of teenage hormones and having never learned effective communication or healthy boundaries was toxic. It seemed I could do no right by her and was regularly punished with severe mental abuse. After spending time with my new friends, I returned home and life soon changed course again. My mother informed me that a man I had once met in the Okanagan had phoned. Looking back I have no idea why she told me and encouraged me to reconnect. I was a child and he was a grown man eleven years my senior. Our reconnection saw me easily fall into the old habits of a lifestyle I was trying so hard to leave behind. I was attending school, trying to live a normal grade nine student life by day, but on weekends my mother would drive me to meet and spend nights at a nearby hotel. The nights were fueled with binges of cocaine, liquor, and inappropriate sex. Not understanding what real love was at age fifteen and growing up with an extremely dysfunctional family, I believed him when he said he loved me, would keep me safe and that we would create a life together. My mother encouraged this relationship and I finally had her approval; I thought that I was the luckiest girl in the world to be wanted and loved by my twenty-six-year-old boyfriend who vowed to love and protect me forever. I believed that I could finally have a *normal* happy, healthy life. If only I had been raised with healthy boundaries and introduced to healthy relationships, I would have been able to see that this relationship and my mother's encouragement was wrong on every level. Not surprisingly, I became pregnant at sixteen and went on to be an unwed mother to three beautiful children by the age of twenty-two. I struggled through a decade of trying to make our very unhealthy relationship work and create the family I desperately wanted yet never had. Despite my wants and efforts, I was fighting against his demons, addictions, dysfunction, abuse, and the fact that I was a child married to a grown man. I knew I needed to be and do better for myself and my children. I continued to search for a path to achieve a better life although I wasn't quite sure what better really was. How does someone who has been raised with very unhealthy, unclear, and non-existent boundaries self-learn things one should have started learning right from infancy? I certainly didn't know but I made it my mission.

I read books, attended parenting classes, went to workshops, saw counsellors, and did any and everything I could think of. I worked hard at school knowing education was key and graduated with the Top Science Student Award. I learned how to set, assess, and reassess my goals. I was determined that every baby step would lead me to the next. I looked to people I respected and tried to emulate them. I was blessed to have an amazing aunt, who taught me to cook, bake, make all kinds of crafts, and explore the beautiful world around me all while helping me to believe in myself and God. I began writing as I felt an internal power surge in my words; it brought clarity to my mind, eased some of the shame I carried, and allowed me an outlet to sort through the chaos that was swirling in my head.

I felt I was worthy of something bigger and better than what I had lived through for so many years.

Growing up amongst all the dysfunction, abuse, and mental illness, took a heavy toll on me. I became a professional chameleon, adapting to whatever environment I was in, for my own mental and physical safety. Although I knew the abuse was wrong, I would silently participate and pretend it didn't happen, and even allowed it as I had been groomed into believing that the road of least contention was the safest path. It took years of continuous effort and a concrete decision that I would no longer put up with abuse from anyone ever again. I eventually learned to set healthy boundaries, though I quickly discovered this caused much animosity among those who wanted me to stay a victim. I was determined and would stop at nothing to break free and rise above.

Later in life, predators would smell the wounds that radiated from me, and dysfunction would, on occasion, rear its ugly head. As I shifted from a victim to a woman of strength who would no longer be silenced, I began rising above all that held me captive for so long. The feeling was both terrifying and exhilarating as a new world of opportunities and adventures opened before me. I feel that I am a true warrior who is deserving, strong, beautiful, courageous, powerful, and filled with so much light, love, and joy. I am a better version of myself each and every day. I had the choice to be the victim or to be my own heroine; I chose the latter. It took much of my life to realize that everything I needed was already inside of me. I just needed to create the safe space, time, understanding, and devotion to myself, before I was able to listen to *her*. My inner voice believed in me and guided me. My new found strength, resilience and confidence, would soon have to face unimaginable pain and suffering, that left me on death's doorstep fighting for my life, in my next chapter as I joined the military. But this time my inner voice and I were better prepared for the battles that lay ahead . . .

Like a work of art, there are many layers, textures and nuances to the lessons I have learned. In allowing others to hear our story, we can collectively break stigmas, lose shame, rise above the ashes, and live an empowered, purpose driven life.

CHAPTER TWELVE

Where's the Silver Lining?

"In the darkest of nights, if you look close enough you can always find a sliver of light. Look for it and embrace the beauty of its shadows."

STEPHANIE REID

Throughout Stephanie's life, she has struggled with mental illness, including depression, anxiety, and PTSD. She learned to suffer through it silently, only ever asking for help when things got too overwhelming to manage alone. She went through therapy here and there, compared herself to everyone she thought had it all together, and wished more than anything that she could change her circumstances. It wasn't until her two-year-old daughter was diagnosed with cancer that Stephanie realized her perspective was completely backward.

In a second, Stephanie would take the pain of her daughter's cancer diagnosis away, but she would never take away the lessons she has learned from it. This is her journey and how she learned how to surround herself with happiness, laughter, and a tribe while watching her daughter fight for her life.

stephaniereid@rogers.com

If you asked me when I was growing up if I would ever be able to embrace and be proud of my mental illness, I would have stared at you with a perplexed and frustrated look that shouted, "Are you fucking kidding me?" Why would anyone ever thank their mental challenges? Why would one embrace the very thing that causes them difficulty and such intense pain? Why would you let it win?

If you told me that my intuition would become so strong that it would never let me fail, I would have thought you were crazy. If you told me that my tribe, the very people who would guide me through the toughest of journeys, would grow with each experience, I would have laughed. I thought I knew it all, that I understood what I was going through and that I should do it alone. I was the only one who understood my pain. Most importantly, though, if you had told me I would finally find myself through one of my most painful lessons, I might have hated you because I wasn't ready to hear it. Today I'm writing a chapter in a book about it. Today I can laugh about the challenges. Today I'm proud to say that my mental illness helped shape me into the mother, wife, and woman I am. I've realized I needed to go through those moments of darkness because I had taken for granted everything my life was offering.

I never knew how strong I was until I was watching my daughter fight for her life. I never thought I would ever thank cancer for anything, but I do. Life handed my daughter the most intense challenge of her life, which in turn possessed me with the strongest will to survive imaginable. If you have ever been told that your child is fighting for their life, you will understand the feelings. If you haven't, I pray to whatever god or ideology you believe in that you never will. Imagine the most painful thing you have felt, add shock, fear, anxiety, disassociation, and debilitating guilt, and multiply it by a thousand. Everything you know to be true is gone in an instant, and you have no way to change it. Who you were a second ago is no longer there (I would later realize this would become a good thing). I truly believe there are pivotal moments in one's life that can change our future for better or for worse: it's all in how you look at it. Will you give it the power to destroy you or will you empower it to lift you up? My daughter's diagnosis put my life into perspective. In an instant, it made me a better person. I became more empathetic and thankful, less judgemental, and I realized that to come out of this journey "sane," I needed to surround myself with other people who were walking this path. I needed to let go of a lifetime of fears of failure, speaking up, and rejection. I needed to find my voice to advocate for my daughter(s) and myself. We would no longer be just a "number" in a system; we have voices and they were going to be heard.

* * *

On Sunday, February 24th, 2013, my daughter Keaton was diagnosed with cancer. She was two years old. My husband and I were worrying about how we would pay for the recently over-flowed toilet when the doctors walked in.

"I'm so sorry; your daughter has cancer."

Anything said after that was inaudible. Time froze in one of the most painful moments I have ever experienced. I remember hearing my husband's tears hit the floor. The sound of every drop silenced my thoughts for a second, and then it hit me. *I did this.* We created this beautiful baby, and look at what we caused. I gave her cancer! You see, when I was seven months pregnant with Keaton, I had overwhelming anxiety about leukemia. I worried day and night for about a month about my daughter getting cancer. I went to my OBGYN, only to be rightfully told, "the pregnancy brain has a way of playing tricks. You've likely seen a commercial for SickKids." Still, I would sit and cry while my oldest napped; after I put her to bed, I would beg God, Buddha, Allah, anyone out there to stop this from happening. "Don't allow my unborn baby to get cancer. Please. I will do anything."

You see, I grew up surrounded by *The Secret*, the idea that what we believe comes true. There I was, absolutely unable to get over the idea that my child could possibly develop cancer; and here she was today, diagnosed with cancer. Talk about overwhelming guilt. I caused this. I believed it, so it must have come true.

Hour after hour. Day after day. They poked my daughter like an endless pin cushion. Hour after hour, day after day, I became a shell of myself. Everything I had to give, I gave to her and like most parents, I would have given anything to switch places with her. I would have sold my soul to the devil to give her an ounce of freedom from this. But I couldn't, so I held it all in, silently and alone. Throughout this journey, I found moments when I could have succumbed to the anxiety; I could have let my fear of the worst possible outcome take over, but I couldn't let it win. I had too much at stake.

One night, though, I allowed myself the time to grieve. I allowed the darkest emotions to take over. Alone, cold, and away from my daughter, I laid on the floor in the hospital's bathroom curled up in the fetal position. I cried in four-hour increments, pausing only twice when the nurses came in to check on Keaton. I gave in. I allowed myself the power to demolish. I listened to my body and gave in to what it needed; and in that moment, I realized for the first time that I held the power—I was the one in control—I would not allow my emotions to control me. Months ago, before Keaton was born, I had already worried about it; I had already prepared myself for this moment, I had already let it overtake me. I looked up, swollen, cold, and exhausted, and said, "Pick yourself up off the floor and get back out there. You can do this!" So I did!

I wish it was that simple. I wish life only handed us one test, one time when we had to face the most horrible feelings and atrocious emotions, only one life lesson that would give us all the knowledge and reminders we need to succeed through every life test. One time to deal with the pain of a challenge. But it doesn't. Life can't. We get too comfortable and we have to be reminded of our morals, our beliefs, our strengths, and the very things that mean the most to us. Life can be taken away in a moment, so it should be cherished, and we must be reminded of what we really want. We must go through these tests.

* * *

When our daughter received the diagnosis, my husband, Don, and I had only been married for three years, although we had been together for over ten. We already had a beautiful four-year-old daughter Mika, and Don had a sixteen-year-old son. Life was busy.

Life was chaotic. Honestly at the time, it seemed not very enjoyable most days. Kids are a lot of work. Who knew? But add in a critically ill child and bam . . . life shows you actual chaos. Life has a way of reminding us that what we thought was hard could be even harder. One night after a very long day of chemo, steroid rage, taking care of a four-year-old, cooking endless meals to provide for Keaton's intense steroid appetite, Don and I got everyone settled and had a chance to blow up on each other. The stress of everything going on had caught up with us. We fought like we had never fought before. The words that came out of our mouths, things I could have never imagined either of us saying, were being said. The cons of staying together seemed astronomical and overwhelming. This would never work. Why are we even going to keep doing this?

And there it was. Divorce. The worst outcome a young married couple rarely thinks about was happening. *Let's end this now before it gets worse.* Both of us went to bed. It was over. It hadn't even really started, but it was over. It was better this way. We slept in separate beds. I "knew" with every ounce of my soul that this was the right decision. But then something amazing happened. I woke up out of a dead sleep. Something shook me. There it was again: the reality of losing. The reality of letting something else win. Cancer was trying to take my daughter, and now it was trying to take my marriage. I could not let it win. I was reminded that I was stronger than this. I had the power to fight this, the power to overcome the anxiety of failure and the resentment of losing what was comfortable, and to take back my power to evaluate what was really going on. I was scared shitless and I felt so alone. I needed to find people who understood this. I needed other warrior moms who could understand my anger and fear. I was mad at my husband, and I was fucking mad at cancer. So began my path to finding my tribe of cancer moms, the strongest women I would know, who would help guide me.

Don and I have just celebrated nine years of marriage. Nine years of difficulties and trials. Nine years of getting to know each other even more. We've gone through hell, and so we celebrate the trials. We celebrate the milestones and moments of laughter. We celebrate the fact that we passed life's test.

* * *

As I reflect on my life and where I am physically, I often thank the challenges I have had placed in our path. It's all about perspective. It's all about how you allow yourself to look at the problem facing you. Will you take it and run, or will you grab the issue and empower yourself to get to know all about it? Don and I became stronger through cancer. So for that, I can thank it.

Over the years, I have been diagnosed with depression, postpartum depression, anxiety, and PTSD, just to name a few. And I will be controversial here and say: I LOVE LABELS. I love that doctors have told me what my "blessings" are. At one time, I would have called them problems, but today I call them blessings. After Keaton's diagnosis, I learned how to label and empower my diagnosis, so that I could navigate her illness with as much positive power as I could. My *depression* forced me to look at my life, and caused me to realize all that I had to be grateful for as well. It showed me all the beauty I had surrounding me because I stopped focusing on everything my depression told me I didn't have. I just needed to look at my life more closely.

If we didn't have something positive, I found it. If we needed laughter, we watched hours of goat and cat videos, anything to make us laugh. If we felt like we needed love, we would surround ourselves with our cancer friends or I would become vulnerable and open up emotionally on Keaton's Facebook page: Kisses for Keaton.

While going through the first couple of months of treatment and secluding myself, my *postpartum depression* made me realize that I needed a "village" filled with moms who were also struggling. It forced me to get out there and find moms who understood what I was going through. It forced me to talk to other moms who felt the same way, so both of us knew we were not alone. It made me realize that as women and moms, we need to empower, surround, and lift up our sisters because we are all in need of a tribe. We are all in need of support.

I am raising two daughters, two beautiful young girls who will one day feel the pressures of being a woman and possibly a wife or mother, too. They will feel the pressures of being perfect and having it all together. They will compare themselves to their peers and girls they see as "perfect." My postpartum depression taught me that I *never* want them to feel alone or less than anybody else.

My *anxiety* showed me the mother I want to be. The mother I want my girls to see. When Keaton lost her hair because of chemo, I shaved my head. I didn't want her to feel alone. I didn't want Mika to think hair defined her. I wanted to understand how my daughters felt and saw the world. I wanted every young woman I met in the oncology unit to know that I saw them. I could understand a little bit of what they felt. I couldn't take the pain away, but I could help them feel a little less alone. I wanted my girls to see that beauty comes from the inside. I wanted them to see the beauty in sheer vulnerability. Even today in the moments when I fail, I still am reminded that I want to strive to be this mother.

I have also given my *PTSD* a platform. It has taught me to speak up and advocate for myself and what I need. It caused me to step out of my comfort zone and seek help when I was in the darkest and deepest of holes. It showed me that when you can't conquer your mental trials yourself, you need to ask for help.

* * *

One day, not too long ago, I broke. Everything I thought I was, everything I thought was safe, wasn't. I was scared to be with my children for fear of hurting them, scared to be without my girls because they represented my comfort, extremely terrified to be alone because of who I had become. The extreme feelings of guilt, rage, and sadness took over again and I realized in that moment that I could no longer live the way I felt. It was either end it all by ending my life or end it all by taking my life back. Everything I had pushed down and hidden behind my smiles and laughs, and the facade of "holding it all together" finally came apart at the seams. Like I said before, just as you get comfortable in life, it has a way of reminding you that all of this can be taken away if you don't constantly check in with yourself. Keaton was six months in remission, so I should have been on top of the world. What was wrong with me? I, again, picked myself up off the floor—literally—and drove myself to the Center for Addictions and Mental Health (CAMH), and begged for help. I sat in the emergency department and told them, "I'm scared. I can't do this alone." Ironically, though, this reminded me that I can do it. I did it. I drove myself to the hospital, I went alone, and I faced my fears. I surrendered to the pain and said, "Nope. No more." I will win.

Through all of my mental illness and challenges, all of Keaton's and Mika's struggles, I have learned one of my most important lessons: advocating. I learned how to publicly speak up, and became a voice for the littlest warriors, the children affected by childhood cancer. I become an ambassador for Camp OOCH (a camp for children affected by cancer), and have spoken throughout various news outlets, both print and TV, to ensure that everyone understands how invaluable support, joy, laughter, and love are when you are struggling. I have watched my daughter laugh through chemo, seen her run and sing while "poison" is being injected into her body. My daughters have reminded me that while our struggles seem huge, there's always someone out there that needs help more. Find them. Help them and speak up for them. I promise you, your problems will slowly become easier to manage.

I understand that my depression, anxiety, and PTSD may seem like they have been easy for me to overcome. Time has healed the rawness of the wounds. Time has allowed me to see every pain and every struggle more clearly. Time has allowed me to gather tribes, and it has helped me seek and welcome wisdom from others who are walking a similar path. Time has shown me that we are not alone; we just need to pick ourselves up off the floor, seek what we need, and speak up for what we deserve.

I know that when one gets depressed, anxious, or is struggling to balance the reality of what you feel with what is really going on, it can seem astronomical. I have been there. I have been faced with the most intense judgement possible while trying to keep our daughter alive. I've questioned and blamed my daughter's cancer on myself. I have created scenarios in my head, and I understand the hell of all of these emotions. I get it.

But more importantly, I have learned to laugh through the tears and I have found my passion through it.

CHAPTER THIRTEEN

Fear: The Bottom Feeder

*"Fear held me captive for so long that
when I finally broke free, those around me
didn't recognize me anymore."*

KADY ROMAGNUOLO

KADY ROMAGNUOLO

Kady Romagnuolo is a mindset and performance coach who specializes in helping clients work through fear and low self-confidence. As a board certified NLP Master Practitioner and Quantum Change Process™ Practitioner, her techniques involve accessing the root cause behind limiting beliefs and negative emotions. Her passion as a coach comes from a place of experience. Kady grew up in a low income suburb of Calgary that was quite rough. Her childhood experiences left her hiding behind the mask of a successful Realtor® while concealing her extreme low self-confidence and constant fear that she wasn't good enough.

Today Kady is a recognized professional in her industry. Her workshops and breakthrough programs help individuals conquer self-doubt and to reach their highest potential. As a motivational speaker, she helps others to engage their core story and embrace change from within. She lives on the waterfront in a country estate on the outskirts of Kingston, ON with her husband and two dogs.

www.kadymindsetcoach.com
ig: @kady.romagnuolo | fb: @kadymindsetcoach | li: @kady-romagnuolo

"Everything you want is on the other side
of fear." -Jack Canfield

I grew up in a rough, low-income suburb of Calgary, Alberta where many people around me became addicts or didn't live past the age of twenty. Living in this setting and going to one of the worst rated high schools in Calgary was difficult and as a result, I had very low expectations of what life could be. You had to be very careful about who you associated with. As the first two years of high school faded away, I noticed my childhood friends starting to act more and more like the stereotype of the neighborhood: drinking, doing drugs, fighting, threatening people they didn't like, and becoming people with no real future.

The problem was if you didn't fit in, you were a target. I hated the idea of spending a Saturday night at a house party where you were sure to end up seeing some bloody fight. I agreed to be a designated driver one night just so everyone would stop asking me to partake in all of the drinking and drugs. As I sat on the couch quietly waiting for everyone else to be ready to leave, I started to draw the attention of a few girls. Apparently, they didn't like that I was not doing what they were doing and started calling me out on it. "What, you think you're too good for us, you stupid B*&#@?" they snarled at me from across the room. These were not people I could have a logical discussion with and explain that I wanted a future, and that what they were doing would not bring me that future I imagined. I managed to leave without incident, but that was one of the few times. During those high school years, other kids physically assaulted me frequently. I once gained the nickname "scarface" for six months after someone took a chunk out of my face because I stood up for someone who didn't deserve what was happening to them. I never actively got into fights with people: I just stood in front of someone who was about to be pummelled and bore the brunt of it. I found myself unable to just stand by, but I learned very quickly that if you spoke up, you would pay.

* * *

As an adult, I started to not speak up for fear of judgement and retaliation, and that mindset of struggling just to survive each day translated into extreme anxiety. I became a master at hiding my nervousness and lack of self-confidence. I thought that if I pretended to be okay, eventually things would get better. It terrified me to express how I actually felt. Somewhere along the line, my experiences had led me to believe that being unsure of yourself or being nervous meant you were weak, and in my surroundings back then, you did not want to appear weak.

On the outside, I had a good job, a wonderful husband, and a beautiful home. But secretly I wasn't sleeping and lived in constant fear that someone would find out about my anxiety, and that I was struggling so badly. There was a voice in my head that I just couldn't stop. The chatter had nothing good to say. I would replay moments of the day on repeat in my mind, thinking about all the things I "should" have said or did but hadn't. I hated myself for it, but didn't know how to change. The only thoughts I knew how to have were those of doubt and worry.

I continually seemed to be in situations in which I did not receive recognition for my hard work. My relationships would fall short of my expectations yet I would find myself with the same type of person again and again. I now believe that the people and experiences that show up in one's life are not coincidence. A pattern emerges if you look closely and will continue until you gain an awareness of why it's presenting.

* * *

In 2017, an opportunity came up for me to attend a real estate conference. As a top producing Realtor® who had nearly a decade of experience, you'd think a conference would be a natural place for me to be. The truth was that the thought of attending gave me so much anxiety that I could barely breathe. Being in a setting with other successful professionals actually triggered my worst thoughts about myself. Unspoken words consumed me when the option of doing anything unfamiliar presented itself. *I'm not good enough to be there. What if I don't know what to say? I don't fit in; these people are all better than me. Who am I? I am no one.* I watched those around me reach their goals with confidence, but never thought this was a reality that I could achieve. I would say to myself, "I bet they never feel nervous or anxious."

In the back of my mind, I was excited to attend this conference, but thoughts of doubt and worry about how I would look or sound clouded my judgement. The need to portray myself as a confident professional ironically fueled my decision to go. Despite my discomfort, the cycle of not wanting to let anyone down forced me to go, and synchronicity took hold. I went to a breakout session where I connected with two trainers who I could have sworn were speaking directly to me in this large group. This gave me a nudge to speak up. *Maybe they would understand?* It took me all day to work up the courage to start a casual conversion with one of the trainers during a break. I couldn't even tell you today what I said in that first conversation; I was in my head so much about how I should stand up straight and make eye contact that I have no idea which words actually made their way out. The only thing I remember for certain is the way I felt when I finally said out loud, "I'm really struggling with anxiety." The words came with tears, shame, and guilt.

The months that followed were challenging. I worked through the voices in my head that were holding me back, the lies that had been running for thirty years. Many were not my own but rather those passed on from my surroundings, from the fear and survival mode that made up my childhood. I realized that my success was being determined by the way others made me feel. In the past, I had felt unworthy, incapable, and undeserving because I was constantly surrounding myself with people who had a reason for me to fail. When I stopped letting others decide who I was and what I was capable of, I learned that I was so much more than I ever thought and that I was not confined by my current job title or my past. By paying attention to the emotions I was feeling instead of pushing them away, I stopped avoiding the real issues and gained an understanding of my core values. While looking for a solution to my anxiety, I found confidence, joy, balance, strength, and gratitude for the experiences of my past. The first step was acknowledging that something had to change, speaking up to say that I needed help and that I didn't know how life could be any different.

A profound thing happens when you follow the signs, the small moments that I call breadcrumbs. On their own, each is just a tiny piece, but together they are complete. I am now more whole while still working toward my ultimate balance, and I am joyful while doing it.

During my search for that strong, independent girl who would stand up to anyone, I was surprised at how much my outward demeanor changed. A few people who knew me during the "dark night of the soul" years, the years when I had lost my spark for life, when I was just going through the day-to-day motions, have reached out to say how different I am now. They said the aura and energy around me is that of a totally different person. They described the person they knew before as cold and reserved, and the person in front of them now as vibrant, bubbly, and energetic. At first I was shocked to hear how I used to appear to others. Then I realized that it made perfect sense. I had been trying so desperately to appear calm, confident, and assertive, but instead I came off as rude and unfriendly. No matter how hard I tried to hide what I was actually feeling, my energy showed the truth. Fear affects us all differently. For me, it took me so far off course that I forgot who I really was. It kept me small and silent. It crippled my confidence and self-worth.

* * *

Now, as a Certified Neuro Linguistic Programming Master Practitioner, I can work through fear when it rears its ugly head. My intention for my professional training as a practitioner and coach was to help myself, and boy, did I ever! I gained the ability to understand where my pain originated. Exposing the truth at my core left me open to forgiving myself for the habits I had picked up and repeated throughout my life. Toxic behaviours were identified and transformed. My self-talk changed from words of negativity and judgement to those of love and encouragement. I learned that forgiving the people of my past was not about saying that what they did was okay. Rather, it meant that I could understand the place of pain that many of them were in and that their actions just repeated that cycle of hurt. Each time I made a breakthrough, I realized that it had all tied back to the level of terror I felt as a child. My fearful experiences had shaped my view of the world and how I felt I would fit into it.

The best thing I ever did was decide to stop feeding the lie that I was not good enough. In fact, I had such tremendous success that other people started to notice, and asked if I could help them too. Sometimes the most worthwhile lessons in life rise out of the hardest struggles. I am so honored today to use my path to show others how they can overcome anything they put their heart and mind to. Your focus is where your future lies so pay close attention to what you're focusing on. I now look back without the deep emotion of regret, and instead feel grateful. Steve Jobs once said, "You can't connect the dots looking forward; you can only connect them looking backwards. So you have to trust that the dots will somehow connect in your future."[1] I couldn't help others to know how to move through pain without first experiencing it myself. I wouldn't have the deep understanding of my life's purpose without trying new things, without failing and picking myself back up again.

* * *

It's never too late. If all you have is one more day, wouldn't you want tomorrow to be great?

My favorite resource, the one that I first started with when my anxiety was at its highest, is what I call the one-minute movie. It's an NLP tool that's simple yet highly effective. How many times have you worried about a particular situation or upcoming event? Like me, you're probably unintentionally running a disaster film about it in your mind, the worst case scenario. Society hasn't done us justice; we've been programmed to plan for the worst. When you plan for the worst, though, where is your focus? It's definitely not the result you want. Next time you catch yourself running all of the terrible outcomes that could happen, stop and think about what you actually want to happen: the best possible version. Then close your eyes and imagine yourself there. Looking through your own eyes—what is happening? Bring it to life in vivid color. When I

---

1   Jobs, Steve. 2008. "2005 Stanford Commencement Address." Stanford University, California. YouTube. May 14, 2008Stanford University. Retrieved from https://www.youtube.com/watch?v=Hd_ptbiPoXM

have a big speaking engagement, I do this for days leading up to the event. I imagine that I'm looking out into the audience, confidently communicating what I'm there to teach. Their faces are observant and focused. I see everything happening in my mind as if I were there now, all unfolding as I want it to. What are the events leading up to that successful moment? I visualize completing all the steps leading up to the event. Do this exercise for one minute and repeat it whenever you catch yourself feeling anxious or worried. It's also a valuable tool to use right before you go to sleep; it will help to release the tension attached to negative thoughts and allow you to sleep more easily.

If you, too, have struggled at any point with anxiety, know that you are not alone. You are supported by something greater and you were meant for more. The world needs you as you are. I thought for a long time that I needed to change something about who I was to be successful, happy, and fulfilled. What I actually needed was to release the anchor of lies I had held onto. I was always enough: I was just hiding behind a wall of fear.

CHAPTER FOURTEEN

Polarities & Chaos: Dancing with a Bipolar Mind

"To scream, not necessarily cause a halt, but an opportunity for a change of course, a connection to another, a break from the isolation, the pain of the mind, the addition of gray: an insertion to the black and white. Truthfully, although this is as difficult to write as it is empowering, necessary, liberating, exciting, terrifying . . . and a mass of other great polarities."

MANDY KARPOFF

MANDY KARPOFF

Mandy Karpoff was diagnosed with a manic depressive disorder in her teens, and has either self-medicated or been on and off medication for the bulk of her life. Nearing her thirties came a second diagnosis of Borderline Personality Disorder; she used reading, writing, meditation, mindfulness practice, open communication, art, and creativity to help her on a daily basis, as well as watching her diet and exercising regularly.

She learned to "ride the waves," manage her symptoms and emotions, all while still experiencing life. These diagnoses will not define me. Mandy is in her tenth year of running her business, Plush Floral Studio, in Burnaby, BC. She is a mother to a beautiful thirteen and a half-year-old daughter, and proud owner of two little dogs.

Mandy has learned to enjoy downtime and relaxation, utilize her energy and creativity, and recognize her triggers and ride out her emotions. She is now nearing her thirty-seventh birthday and has been unmedicated for just over two years. She hopes that her story will help people who are in different stages of their lives, as so many courageous people helped her along her journey.

Plushfloralstudio.ca | www.messymind.ca
ig: @mandy_mandy_333 | @plushfloralstudio
fb: @mandy karpoff | li: @mandy karpoff | t: @plushfloralstudio

On my "good" days, which are maybe my manic days, depending on your position of judgement or perspective, I sit at a mantle and perform a series of motions and mantras, while the world is asleep, inclusive to expressing gratitude for my hands, my fingers, and all that they do. Think, if you lose one, or more, how life would change. Think of all the places they have been and have yet to go, all the work and all of the tasks they perform with discipline. They tip-toe cautiously, curiously, task orientated, focused, with precision and with grace. Doing exactly as I tell them, no back talk, no eye rolling, no passive-aggressive comments. Enthusiastically, wholeheartedly. As if fingers have hearts.

I have wanted, for as long as I can recall, to write a book. It is nearly an impossible task to organize the chaotic thoughts and this loopy and swirling maze that is my mind. And so I will go with it and I will start here. Thanks for reading.

I bought four huge watermelons accidentally on purpose, at four in the morning while performing an online grocery shop, in hopes of avoiding a trip to the supermarket and the amount of time this would dissolve, in the peak of a bipolar manic phase. I was sure I would make all the previously found recipes and still make it to the gym for seven. I was embarrassed when the watermelons arrived, and was not sure how to explain them to my daughter and my then-boyfriend, so I utilized humor, brushing it off externally while simultaneously resenting the both of them for laughing at me internally. Irony, separated from what I do or how I appear, versus what is going on inside and the fear of how I feel. Prompted by a belief that I am in this alone, that I have to defend and hide my strange behavior from everyone, that they will not love me anymore, that I will be found out, lose everything; perhaps this is an example of the paralyzing and isolating black-and-white thinking said to be characteristic of Borderline Personality Disorder.

This shopping excursion occurred near the end of my raw vegan phase. It ended in what felt like thousands of dollars worth of raw cashews that I had been soaking, inevitably forgotten, accidentally on purpose. Perhaps admitting this is, in a way, embracing the self-sabotage or allowing my brain to get busy and get lost somewhere, anywhere other than here. A skill on one hand, but sometimes when I forget I am doing it, a bad habit. So the raw vegan phase ended in this mass of forgotten (golden cored) cashews, steamily put to rest in my trash can, warmed in thick black pubic hair-looking mold. Reminded me of my ex. One of the first. Twenty years ago and ten years my senior. His body hair. Dark, intimidating, secretive. A reminder that he is a man. Total opposite of me. I had nowhere to hide. In later days, he would compulsively remove his hair. In an attempt to get clean. From the outside in. The cocaine days.

Clean. Cleaner. Less complicated. Easier to see. Less room to hide. Even from yourself. But it is easier and more tangible to start from the outside, tangible to-do lists, climaxed in a check. "Try to start inward," I tell myself. I learn with time. That's much more difficult. Wash the floors. Shine the mirrors. Empty the dishwasher. Check. Check. Check. Get over the childhood shit. Sort out the dark voices. Get out of bed. Don't break up with anyone today. A little harder to complete. More ongoing, you could say. No spunky, satisfying check mark climax. A process. Of practice, not perfect. Of learning and unlearning. Birth and rebirth. Light amongst the cracks.

I bought a food dehydrator after the all-red-meat-and-animal-fat-everything diet. After the juice cleanse. That ended in pizza. That night-capped in laxatives. When the lithium didn't work. When I decided I wasn't in fact an alcoholic. Should I go for a run or go for a smoke? Weight train or do yoga? Meditate or drink wine? I suppose this is more of the black-and-white thinking they talk about. Feels a little more grey and spectrum–ish to experience; and when you are in it, it is harder to find the perspective, so sometimes it is blotchy and pulsating red, a prayer for black and white.

"What is it like to have bipolar?" asks my daughter. "It isn't your fault," says boyfriend number thirty-nine. Post-body hair. "Do you really think there is such a thing as a personality disorder?" my cousin quizzes.

"And if that which you seek to find, within yourself you never find it without." This has become an important chant in a series of rituals and poems ingrained in my brain, written on my wall, mismatched mantras and quotes from various reads and discussions over the years. In between tastes of tarot, dances with Buddhism, a mosaic of spiritual practises and learning. To try to soften the Catholic guilt from childhood. Helpful when I can remember to practice and step forward. It is not about finding the answer in others, but within. The soul speaks. It is quiet sometimes. And doesn't speak in words. The magical mystery game we call life. Like dancing. Playing. I can't give up yet; the song is not over. And there will be other songs. It is about listening to the beat, the beat that speaks to me, the one you can find in my veins, and letting it drain into my heart and pulse out into the world. Swirl of red to a million other colors, and relish in the process. Even when the color is barf green. Or even black or white.

The more I control things (or try to), the less open to possibilities I am. Sometimes I feel so stuffy and claustrophobic; like someone is sitting on my neck and pressing their heel into my heart and I cannot breathe; like those dreams where you cannot scream. Even though you're falling. Even though he's stabbing. If I could only just scream. Make it all stop.

And then I decided that this is not a dream, and I can scream. To scream, not necessarily cause a halt, but an opportunity for a change of course, a connection to another, a break from the isolation, the pain of the mind, the addition of gray: an insertion to the black and white. Truthfully, although this is as difficult to write as it is empowering, necessary, liberating, exciting, terrifying . . . and a mass of other great polarities. As is life. Where once I felt self-hatred, rage, and an overwhelming sense of not wanting to be here, not wanting to be diagnosed with these things, I now feel hopeful, loved, and connected. Purposeful. Suicide is actually off the table, when once it was a thought-out plan B.

It's not always positive, rarely easy. But there is this belief in change, and fluidity, and grace. An acceptance. A practice of mindfulness. *Mindfulness for Borderline Personality Disorder* by Blaise

Aguirre and Gillian Galen is a terrific and super helpful read with simple exercises on mindfulness practise (I would recommend). I still have dark days, engage in destructive behaviors or let impulse drive, and fall into old patterns. But they are no longer worth ending it all in my mind; my mind is no longer my enemy. I am in a sense, learning myself and how I am in the world. Simultaneously, this allows for me to learn and relate to others and to sustain an abundance of compassion, and a belief and faith in the absolute that this too shall pass: the good and the bad, the ups and the downs. Through acceptance, through time, through an acceptance of time, and continued learning and a commitment to not give up; I learn to ride out the dark times, name my triggers, take naps, allow myself to be vulnerable, and share my chaos. Not everyone will like me, or this, and I too, will not always like myself, the experiences I encounter, the people I cross paths with. But I choose to see it as a learning experience, and feel grateful.

On suicide—idealization, planning, the spiraling thoughts that are no longer on the table for me—I would like to share something from *The Buddha and the Borderline* by Kiera Van Gelder. The author is recalling an experience when she is learning about Buddhism, and she asks her teacher about suicide in relation to the practice of non-violence to others. "Is suicide the same as hurting someone else?" she asks. He responds, "Yes. If you understand that killing in any form results in great suffering, why would you choose to kill yourself . . . it is like scratching an itch with a knife, karmically speaking, there is no relief . . ." What a simple, beautiful, thought-provoking, and perspective-shifting statement. Acceptance of the thought, mindfulness, and "proceeding with caution." I am not cured, but I believe I am better able to notice a "symptom" coming up and proceed with tools. As well, with an awareness of my purpose and spot in this world, no matter how little I like it at times. I realize I am important, and that everyone is connected. To harm yourself is in fact to harm others.

I had first been diagnosed with bipolar in my teens, when it was not yet renamed "bipolar," but was called manic depressive disorder. I have since been on and off antidepressants (later, I would learn this can in fact trigger greater bipolar symptoms). I have self-harmed, self-medicated, struggled with addiction to various substances and behaviors, struggled with eating disorders, been in tumultuous relationships, pushed and pulled people in and out of my life, broken my own heart, and shat on anyone who came close to me. I have manipulated and fired many therapists and psychiatrists, taken many different types of medications, including antidepressants galore, anti-psychotics, anti-anxiety meds, and finally lithium. I have fantasized and idealized about and attempted suicide for years, and wanted to give up so, so, so many times. An ex-boyfriend with a heroin and sex addiction who worked in the medical field—after an exhausting evening of "leave, come back, I hate you, don't leave me, don't touch me, hold me closer," another awesome and super helpful read, if you or someone you love is suffering is, *I Hate You Don't Leave Me: Understanding the Borderline Personality* by Jerold J. Kreisman and Hal Straus—came to me in the morning with a dozen-odd pages printed out on Borderline Personality Disorder. It was chilling to read the symptoms: I was nine for nine. I had given up on trying to treat my bipolar symptoms, and had even sort of learned to shelve the very idea that I had it. I would climb onto people and their ideas and projects, cling to them momentarily, and try to watch for their responses, to see if what I was doing was "okay." To see if my behavior was acceptable. I would submerge myself in projects and passions (let's be honest, obsessions). I would work seventeen-hour days and be terrified to sleep, to be calm, to be alone with myself, and with my thoughts, and the panic and pain that would inevitably arise. I could not express how I felt, what I liked, what hurt me, what made me happy. I did not trust who I was, was terrified of her, and would try to grasp for acceptance anywhere. I felt alone and scared, like everyone else in the world had a sort of rule book and knew the code of conduct, and I was some sort of a wild animal with the self-awareness and emotional maturity of a six-year-old.

After another ex-boyfriend told me, "You need help," I went to my doctor. They prescribed me lithium, a psychiatrist, a therapist, and an addiction counsellor. They instructed me to have blood work done weekly to maintain my levels, and make sure that my blood was not toxic. Did I mention I am a single mother to a now thirteen-year-old (with no immediate family in the province) and that I run my own flower shop business (like ALL of it, including the website, photos, paperwork, designs, merchandising, purchasing, marketing, customer service, and often deliveries . . .)?! Lithium killed my creativity and cut me off from my body. It was hard to run a business and raise a child, and actually be there for her (physically present and emotionally in the room experiencing what was going on with her) when I felt so doped up on something to make me "level" or acceptable to society. Not to mention the three trips a week to the mental health ward at the hospital, and blood labs, parking, and traffic. It was physically not something I could keep up with if I wanted to keep my business and be a part of my daughter's life.

But I stayed on lithium for nearly six months. I did notice more space from my thoughts and impulsivity; it gave me clarity and time to notice, observe, and learn some of my (many) triggers and the bad behaviors (often compulsive and rooted in addiction) that I used to cope. I would like to stress that I am far, far, far from "cured," but I feel extensive gratitude that I have been able to learn so much about these deeply rooted patterns and behaviors. How harmful and isolating they are, and have been. I find great comfort (and again immense gratitude) in this light at the end of the tunnel, and my ability to now name my feelings, choose the lens through which I view my experiences. I can experience hurt and pain, and I survive it. The greatest irony is that real life is nothing compared to the self-created pain and discomfort of the chaos and isolation I have spent years in. The thing about mental illness and being diagnosed with something (or many things) is that the outcome is two-fold. I have come to believe that life is all about polarities. Without the moon's reflection, we do not get to see the sun. Without rain, no flowers. What goes up always comes down. My diagnosis has been helpful to me, to label and then learn patterns and characteristics, to connect with others, to hear other's experiences, to learn about how they have survived. It has also been paralyzing when I spend too much time on Google or have a conversation with someone very opinionated and married to their opinions, or when there is too much emphasis placed on the "disorder" and "illness" part.

Another life-changing read for me is *An Unquiet Mind* by Kay Redfield. She openly shares her experiences and life with manic depressive disorder (bipolar). She is a successful (and one of the few) female professors of medicine for American universities, and shares openly about the way this diagnosis, and learning to work

POLARITIES & CHAOS:
DANCING WITH A BIPOLAR MIND

with some of its capacities, has shaped her life. It was incredibly humbling and inspirational, and reached deep into the corners of my heart. For me, the more I can learn, the more I am able to un-attach from the unhealthy. I am able to utilize my mania and not always act on impulsivity.

I believe this life to be fluid, and our experiences are all on a spectrum. I may one day revisit the route of medication. For now, I allow myself to be sad, and I don't beat myself up for it. I speak openly about it, and take space (if I can) so I do not hurt others or make choices out of impulse and emotion. I write a lot. I journal and work things out with myself; sometimes this takes hours, days, pages for me to get to the bottom of what is going on. I recognize that something another person may brush off or not even notice may affect me deeply, and take me a while to work through. With the understanding that I am basically like an exposed nerve with intensified feelings, I have been able to cultivate coping mecha-nisms (for the most part healthy ones, or less destructive than in the past) and build deep connections with others and with myself. To be even more honest, and perhaps this is taboo, I enjoy my manic phases and the expendable energy. I try to remove or limit triggers and chemicals (and even foods, caffeine, etc.) that induce mania, and rather engulf myself in practises of mindfulness. Borderline Personality Disorder to my understanding is a basic un-knowing of oneself. Behaviors are developed as coping mechanisms. Constant desire to fill this feeling of "empty." The practise of mindfulness can allow for self discovery, and slowly I am learning to trust my intuition, even if that trust is in allowing for the possibility that my truth is not necessarily always accurate. I would love to end this, and tell you how healthy and healed and "normal" I have become; instead I struggle with appropriate wording to leave off. I believe that no matter where any of us sit on a spectrum of mental health or dis-ease, it is a forever journey. The greatest gift you can give yourself is compassion and trust. Even when the trust is in the re-alization that you need help. I do not know that I am "recovered," but I feel much progress has been made when I am able to enjoy moments, feel connection, and even laugh at myself. Unhealthy habits still remain, I also notice when I am doing them, and at times am able to go deeper, or practise a certain harm reduction in my destructive behaviors.

If you or someone you know is struggling, I will not state a generic "get help" message. This is so much easier said than done, and something I have heard so many times. I will say, get honest, in the moment, do your best to move past it, to sit with the feelings rather than act on them. Name them, reach out even if it is simply to read a book or touch your feet to the earth. Moods shift, they are impermanent for all of us. The spectrum of severity is heightened with people diagnosed with bipolar disorder. Having faith that this too shall pass, and doing something to pass the time, or shift the perspective (even something as simple as three pages in a journal, a walk around the block, a nap, a face mask, or a phone call to a friend where you practise truly listening to another). A lot of the negative behaviors (or unsavory coping mechanisms developed) are a means of getting out of your own head, so it has been helpful and productive for me to continue to replace this with a more positive behavior. Something as simple as, rather than obsess over a conflict or indulge in negative emotion, find something to be grateful for, or a positive relationship or situation and run with it! It is like getting dressed; and you don't like your ass? . . take up a running program or get a gym membership, and in the meantime dress to accentuate your upper body, and be nice to your ass; as it is a part of you, and also necessary.

CHAPTER FIFTEEN

Empowered Vulnerability

*"By listening to my inner voice, I learned
what to say out loud when I was ready to
no longer be silent."*

KIKI CARR

KIKI CARR

Kiki Carr was born in Ontario, Canada and grew up in a small city east of Toronto. She studied criminology at Ontario Tech University, focusing on domestic violence, women's studies, victimology, and psychology, with the aim of understanding *why people do what they do.* Kiki is an Amazon best selling author and a Book Excellence Award Finalist who focuses on personal development, human interest pieces, mindfulness, and mental health. In 2019, she was first published in a co-authored book, *Unleashing Her Wild*, a collection of stories written by women who have found a deep connection to intuition and instinct. *She's No Longer Silent* is her second coauthor book. As an entrepreneur, Kiki has been featured in *She Does the City*, *East Magazine*, and *Metroland Media;* and has written for Station Gallery, Golden Brick Road Publishing House, *Medium,* and more.

www.kikicarr.com | www.medium.com/@carrkristine
ig: @carrkristine | fb: @carrkristine

For many years, I felt strong enough to speak up and speak out. I knew my voice and didn't feel the need to stay silent. But when you become influenced by a way of thinking, a way of reacting and consequences of standing up among the masses, you systematically start sitting down and keeping to yourself. What others required of me and what others wanted of me was always a different story. I found myself in quarrels, mentally abusive friendships, triangles, arguments over injustices, and overall frustration and confusion, not because of my lack of courage in speaking out but because of the lack of courage of those around me.

"What would people think?" they would ask.

"It's not our responsibility," they would state.

"Don't make this about you," they would interject.

"Why do you always have to stir everything up?" they would accuse.

As time went on, I became silent out of fear of upsetting others. Although it's *my* fear, it was the words and actions of others that created that fear. The result? A shoving down of emotions, thoughts, and feelings, right down into a place where everyone tells me to stay quiet to *keep the peace*. But is it really keeping the peace, or is it a facade?

When I hold things in and push them down, it brews my own special batch of mental illness. The emotions and unspoken words, dashed with a gag order, get stored in my gut and told to stay there. Then the toxic off-gases fume up into my head and start corroding my brain's capacity to function normally. What happens inside of me at these times is silent suffering. If you are speaking out about an injustice or you are speaking your truth, the act of staying silent or silenced can be a prison sentence.

When the idea for this book first came to be, it was to be a safe space for women to have a platform for their voice. The biggest pain that I've suffered mentally has stemmed from the fact that I was alone and silenced by fear. Having these co-authors come together for the purpose of helping others who are struggling to see that they are not alone is the biggest gift any of us could give. The reasons we stay silent may vary, but at the end of the day, keeping it locked away deep down causes suffering. This book is for the reader holding it tightly in their grip, the one who has something to express and the one who feels the depths of their loneliness in it.

You are not alone.

Your emotions are valid and real.

You are welcome here.

You are heard here.

LOOKING TO MYSELF

You would think that the solution to forced silence would be the opposite: speaking very loudly and letting it all go, as a means to clean up the mess. But in fact, this reaction just leaves toxic remnants that are worse than the original emotions. I've learned through my personal journey the importance of empowered vulnerability and the strength that comes with it. Now when I speak up, I speak from a place of power, understanding, and compassion. Rather than let the toxic emotions enter my body, I see them as separate from myself. I acknowledge them, I love them, I allow them to be as they are, and I learn from them. Noticing emotions as they are without trying to change them has been a practice I've learned through mindfulness. Mindfulness is most easily described as noticing something as it is, without judgement. I use this practice in easy and difficult times and use both circumstances to stay grounded, connected, and aware. With that awareness comes empowered decisions. When I can look at a situation without my emotional attachment, I can better serve the task at hand. I can look objectively and shift the perspective from overwhelmed blurting, to proactive solutions. Easier said than done, but that's why it's called a mindfulness practice, and practice makes . . . well, imperfect perfection. And that's perfectly enough.

From a mindful place, I started looking within myself for an-swers rather than to others around me for validation. I looked to my-self and my inner knowing for my voice. In the past, and sometimes still now, I couldn't hear my voice amid my loud disapproval of what was happening, trapped under the screaming emotions in me that wanted to lash out. But by listening to my inner voice, I learned **what** to say out loud when I was ready to no longer be silent.

Becoming no longer silent means verbally speaking up for something, but it also means speaking up for yourself. Listening to yourself and believing in yourself.

> *I look to myself and believe in my words.*
> *I look to myself to be my advocate.*

No one else can soothe my cries like I can. If someone quiets me or prefers me silent, succumbing to that victimization will not serve me, but acknowledging and validating my feelings will. Love for yourself is a powerful tool and it is readily available if you are ready to access it with pure intentions. Love will bring you through all the ups and downs. Love will support you, love will protect you, love will comfort and guide you.

STAYING IN MY LANE

I won't ever please everyone, no matter how hard I try and no matter what I do. Only they can do that for themselves, in the same way only I can for myself. Regardless of being silent or speaking up, we have no control over the perception that people around us will have of us or our actions. What you *do* have control over is *your* perception and *your* actions. What do *you* need? What *inten-tions* do you have? What *emotion* are you speaking from?

Is your desire to no longer be silent coming from a place of em-powered vulnerability or emotionally charged expression? There is no wrong answer. Your best is all that is required of you and if you're doing your best, then you are right where you're supposed to be. But your intention is the secret to how you will feel after you speak. It's your barometer that sets the tone for the aftermath. If your intention is coming from pure love, then the actions that come when you are no longer silent will be your guiding light.

SUPPORT SYSTEMS

Although you are your soul level and your strongest ally, when you are ready to stand up and speak up, there is power in finding support in your community, family, and friends. Be specific and particular. This is not where a numbers game is important, this is where quality over quantity will bring you strength. If you are speaking out on behalf of someone else, ask the person what *they* need, and don't assume you know their best interest. Be sure you are honoring them and supporting them in the way they need.

There are organizations built around helping and guiding people who are struggling, and some are just a phone call away 24/7. It can be the hardest part to just make a phone call and allow sound to come through your mouth, but just start with two letters: *Hi.*

During my worst times of mental illness, I could not find the courage to speak words, and so I stayed silent. Although the silence was crippling, going through my illness alone left me isolated in plain sight. Loneliness as a social being was the pair of hands pulling me down into deep waters, the ones that silence pushed me into. Silence and loneliness walk hand-in-hand, and sometimes you can't tell them apart. When I learned to differentiate between the two and understand why I was being silent, I started to make steps toward not doing it alone.

I started to surround myself with people who will listen, no matter what. If your time is spent with those who don't listen to your words, that's okay. That is their journey, just as this is yours. I don't blame those people, I don't try to change them: I just let them go. They will come back when they are ready.

Then I got even more specific and invited my growth to flourish with people who believe in me and my words. These are not "yes people;" rather, these are advocates who believe in my heart, even when my words don't match up.

Although I was still being silent and silenced, I opened up to a few people whom I knew could handle it and still stay in their own lane, too. Loneliness was caught and held accountable. I saw it for what it was: an unnecessary burden.

The Silver Lining

I'm grateful for my struggles.
I don't invite them back in,
but I see them as lessons to learn if I'm willing to
be a student.
If I had not struggled:
I would not be a published author;
I would not be writing a chapter in my
second book;
I would not be specific about whom I intentionally
surround myself with;
I would not have asked myself every day, "What
brings me joy?"
and I would have settled for a mediocre life.

I was stuck in patterns that kept repeating themselves because I wasn't ready to listen to myself, my inner guidance, or something bigger than me. I wasn't ready to change because fear and struggle was all I knew. I was only able to let go of the struggle of silence and loneliness when I was ready to be grateful for it. Along my journey, I learned that I can heal at the root of pain by having gratitude for its lessons and by sending it the love it needs to move on. Much like a child in pain, our struggles need to be heard, healed, and validated. Your struggle is that child.

She's No Longer Silent

I don't shout from the rooftops,
I don't angrily post my objections on
social media,
I don't argue with the people around me in
"teachable moments,"
and I don't strive to change the world.
I do speak my truth with alignment for my goals,
I do stand in my power,
I do thrive in empowered vulnerability,
and I do wait to see if the person I disagree with is
ready to be a student.
I don't let people walk all over me,
but I do allow them to be who they choose to be.
I stand up and speak out when another person cannot
do it for themselves only when I know they need it
for *them*, not because of my own beliefs.

I thought I needed to fight to save myself and others, but I've found peace in finding my own grounded way to speak up. If I had not struggled and if I had not experienced inner conflict in being silent, I would not have found my gift as a writer and you would not be reading these words. I use my gifts as a writer to be the vessel to speak up, to no longer be silent, and to help others. Instead of constantly being emotionally charged with so much to say, to try and save the world, I lead by example. I do my best to be a light in the dark. I am not right and I am not wrong. I ask for guidance and I listen to its wisdom to formulate the words that can serve others. Although I am no longer silent, I am not noise.

I am no longer silent, but I do not shout.
I am no longer silent,
but I use my intentions to be my voice.
I am no longer silent, and I am free.

CHAPTER SIXTEEN

Healing with Spirits and Energy

"I am grateful for my life because every soul we meet and each experience we have shapes who we are and I can finally proudly say, I like me."

WHITNEY STOUT

WHITNEY STOUT

Whitney Stout is an energy work coach for Trauma Stewards, and staff attorney at South Carolina Legal Services in the USA. Her work includes leading a unit dedicated to tackling implicit bias and the systemic inequities that impact people of color, the LGBTQ+, and limited English-speaking communities. She holds a juris doctor and bachelor of arts degree in psychology and spanish. She is a 2019 Fellow of the Shriver Center Racial Justice Institute.

Whitney is also Reiki certified and taking part in a Shamanic Practitioner Certification program. Her passions for psychology, energy work, and systems thinking led her to develop and offer courses and coaching for individuals to unpack, clear, and heal the biases and toxic patterns limiting them from living their authentic truths.

www.Ethical-Energy.com
ig: @EthicalEnergy | fb: @EthicalEnergy | t: @Ethical_Energy
www.goodreads.com/user/show/108644053-whitney
www.pinterest.com/EthicalEnergy
www.youtube.com/ethicalenergy

I healed my anxiety disorder, but was certain if people found out they would think I was delusional. As a child I was tense, uptight, and high strung. I directed that energy to goals. At an early age, after I abandoned the idea of being Wonder Woman's sidekick, I decided I would be a legal aid attorney or a psychologist. I voluntarily sacrificed my recess so I could stay inside to read and asked my teachers for extra assignments, so I could advance beyond the class material. I took course overloads in college to maximize my academic marketability. My resume building paid off and I was able to get a scholarship for my law school tuition, but struggled to pay my living expenses. I worked while in law school but still graduated with massive debt. The financial pressure of needing to pass the bar exam catalyzed me to snap. I would stare at my study guides literally paralyzed and unable to process the information. Daily stressors like traffic or extra errands would trigger sobs. I made our already tight budget worse, impulse spending on fast food and Amazon trinkets. For some reason with my spouse my anxiety manifested as rage. I yelled, cried, and one day destroyed his beer mug collection. Smashing each one individually for punctuation to that particular day's meltdown. The study window shortened as the bar exam came closer. I was on track to fail the bar exam, and was verbally and emotionally abusing my spouse. At the time it didn't occur to me to see a therapist or treat this as a mental health issue. Law school is meant to be hard. The process was expected to be stressful. Like a culling to see who wouldn't be able to handle the legal field. I believed the feelings would dissipate after the exam and just wanted medication to subdue me until I was done studying. I sought help from a general family medicine practitioner, and received a prescription for anxiety attacks and anger management medication.

After passing the bar I went off the medication, thinking since the test would be over I would be fine. I had difficulty finding a job and went out into business alone. What I didn't fully understand is that as a solo practitioner I wasn't just an attorney, I also had to think like an entrepreneur. Within a year I was bankrupt and my mental health was in shambles. I had no experience with business management, causing me to charge way too little money for my services. I performed work I hadn't been paid for, trusting people would follow through with their payment plans. My financial situation was precarious; if someone was prepared to pay and I was competent to do the work, I accepted the case, even if the client made me uncomfortable. I was putting myself in vulnerable situations thinking my good intentions would protect me. The turning point came during the 2016 presidential election in the United States. I used an office inside of another business in exchange for performing minor administrative work. I primarily practiced immigration law and most of my clients were Spanish-speaking undocumented immigrants. After the results of the 2016 presidential election, the clientele of this business did not want to share a reception area with my clients. The business owner ultimately decided my clients could no longer use the same waiting room as hers. After the election many of my clients ghosted, and no longer wished to pursue their applications. My clients that remained could sense the now open hostility from the clients of the other business and the business owner, and began to feel mistrustful. At the same time I was dealing with a stalker who took an interest after seeing one of my ads. Ultimately for my personal safety I was forced to abruptly leave that office and begin closing down my business. My clients were understandably angry because even if their money was refunded, the next attorney they found would charge significantly more than I had, and many had been unable to hire an attorney previously precisely because of that financial barrier. I ended up having to defend myself against ethics complaints, was followed home, and taken to court. Eventually I found a job as a legal aid attorney, the ethics complaints were resolved, and my practice was closed. I tried to be grateful, but behind closed doors I was dying on the inside. My entire life I had worked towards the goal of being an attorney, and shortly after attaining this goal made very public mistakes. I kept having to explain these mistakes to the attorneys my former clients were trying to hire. Some encouraged me to leave the practice of law, and declared I didn't have what it took to make it in this profession.

I internalized this criticism and began to believe I had no place being an attorney. I felt like a fraud. I was often running late to my new job because I'd start throwing up at the thought of going into the office. When I worked with my door shut it was because I was typing pleadings between sobs. At home I would melt down and hide in the back of my house in a dark room under blankets. The anxiety triggering sensory overload, unable to tolerate the sounds of the road, or little things like my spouse's chewing. I would engage in numbing behaviors to disassociate, begging to not feel, just for a moment. I hated myself for descending into this blackness. At work I saw people everyday overcoming overwhelming obstacles to make their lives better, and to provide for their families. I had a home, a job, a supportive spouse and family, and felt like scum for having these advantages and still wanting to disappear.

I tried to hide the severity of my mental health, but my spouse saw it all. Having overcome his own dark descent before our marriage he knew what it looked like to see someone give up. One day he sat me down and told me that I needed to decide I wanted to feel better. He thought I was engaging in emotional self-harm. He was right. The closure of my practice adversely affected many of my clients and I struggled with accepting I couldn't make it up to them. I would remain the villain in their personal stories. On some level I wanted to be miserable as some sort of karmic penance for my mistakes. He said my loved ones needed me to decide I deserved to be happy.

Healing became my life's work. I started seeing a therapist. I learned the benefit of having a safe neutral space to share with someone who isn't personally vested in my life decisions. Devouring multiple self-help books a week, I discovered the power of learning from someone's first-hand personal experience. I saw myself in their stories. Their stories gifted me the words to name and describe my experiences. I dove deep into the mind-body connection and became a believer in the benefits of meditation. A course in transcendental meditation taught me to observe my feelings, rather than becoming them. The shift from "I am angry" to "I feel anger," and the meditation techniques, helped disrupt the bio feedback loop that fed my anxiety attack cycles. I was healing but then my growth stagnated. I was still experiencing anxiety attacks daily. I still feared taking risks and swam in the great sea of imposter syndrome. I had been diagnosed with Generalized Anxiety Disorder, and with that diagnosis came the caution that I was physiologically imbalanced and would likely remain that way. Anxiety may constantly be something I had to manage. I thought I may need to leave the practice of law, quit my job, in favor of a profession that was less stressful. I was frustrated and wanted to transcend my diagnosis. I traded my self help books for spiritual texts, feeling a call that my life-long love of mythology and world religions could be my map to ascension. I came across a book called *Journey to the Dark Goddess: How to Return to Your Soul* by Jane Meredith. The author observed that our modern society often perpetuates this myth that we should always be striving for "peace" and "positive vibes only," and openness about periods of emotional darkness is something to avoid. I considered the idea that maybe I wasn't broken, but that the dominant cultural narrative simply lacked the tools to assist us in navigating and returning from periods of pain.

I began to rethink my entire mental health diagnosis and the culture of mental health in our society. I learned many ancient shamanistic cultures viewed the manifestation of what we diagnose as mental illness today as someone having a different connection to, and perception of the energetic and spiritual worlds. I was hesitant to embark on a healing journey based on energy work and ancient mythologies. I was afraid I would placebo effect myself into believing a fantasy. Before I could proceed, I wanted some sort of proof that energy work was real. I read the *Holographic Universe* by Michael Talbot, and learned physics has shown us that everything is energy. The book *Vibrational Medicine* by Richard Gerber showed me that Reiki healing, crystal healing, and chakras were all real. I began learning Qi Gong from a massage therapist who was also a meditation coach. She taught me to feel the energy of my natural environment, and how the flow of the energy between the earth, the heavens, and ourselves can empower and heal us. I became certified in Reiki, and the daily Reiki treatments I performed on myself facilitated my anxiety attacks all but disappearing. I saw a local shamanic practitioner for soul retrieval sessions to embrace my personal power and transcend my fear. Experiencing such transformation that I enrolled in a shamanic practitioner training myself. My life was changing, I was healing something I previously thought was a permanent part of my reality.

There is a belief that as more people walk this path of healing a great shift will occur in the collective unconscious of our communities and our world. I began to experience a deep yearning to be part of that shift. To share my light and plant seeds of healing. For years I had stayed silent about this spiritual journey. I wrote online and had formed amazing friendships in the spiritual community under the pen name Lagertha Scarlet. Lagertha, inspired by a legend of a woman who made her potential suitor fight a bear (and the character from the show *Vikings*), and scarlet after an anime warrior wizard.

I was afraid that because I was living in the Christian South my coworkers and community would feel uncomfortable or hostile if I came out as an energy worker. Being open about my mental health spiral could cause my competency to practice law to be questioned, and I was protective of the professional credibility I had so carefully been rebuilding since my business closure three years earlier. Although all cultures across the world have shamanistic roots, I knew some folks considered the practice of modern shamanism a form of cultural appropriation. As the head of race equity initiatives at work, I did not want to appear hypocritical. Above all else I was afraid to admit I healed my anxiety disorder. Health is complex. Everyone's diagnosis, body, heart, soul, and circumstances are different. Saying I healed my mental health diagnosis could be triggering. Would I lose the friendship of my fellow mental health warriors? If I started offering energy healing services would my healer friends feel upset like I was competing with them? Would they feel I had only been using them to gain knowledge to start my own practice? I felt selfish and greedy knowing I had a full-time job and could "steal" sales from someone who may need the money more than me. I wondered if monetizing aspects of my spiritual practice to offer services was imperialistic, and would taint my relationship with spirit. There was also the fact that as I went deeper into my shamanistc practitioner training I began to see and feel spirits and astral entities. That's not stuff everyone is on board with believing, and paired with my anxiety disorder diagnosis could lead some to think I was perhaps unstable. I turned to those very women I was afraid of alienating, and told them my fears and shared my doubts. One after another they added fuel to my inner fire. Not just words of support, but rather shouts of encouragement. One healer shared her belief that each healer operates on a different vibration, from a different space, and the more healers there are, the more likely someone will find the perfect one that resonates with their needs. Another friend felt that in older times people would bring healers and spiritual workers gifts or perform trades, and that the tradition of an energy exchange between healer and client had been a tradition going back centuries, even though now that exchange usually involved cash rather than a barter. My friends in the mental health community were not angry or triggered, but instead encouraged me to launch a coaching business so I could directly help support others in their healing empowerment journey.

I retired my pen name, and merged my mundane world self with my alias Lagertha Scarlet. I started small with coming out at work. I slowly brought in crystals, hung a wall hanging of the egpytian goddess Bast in my office, and started casually bringing up lunar events. The language of energy work is universal. I was able to discuss healing concepts with coworkers who were of a variety of spiritual paths. I've realized that my work as a legal aid attorney, energy worker, healer, and coach are not separate fields at all. They all further the goal of empowering others and shifting patterns and circumstances. When I meet criticism I am grateful because I have crossed paths with a heart that may benefit from the seeds of healing being planted.

I will no longer stay silent because if it hadn't been for the personal stories of others' I would never have embarked on this path. I am grateful for my life because every soul we meet and each experience we have shapes who we are and I can finally proudly say, I like me. Shamans are sometimes referred to as the wounded healers. Only by healing ourselves will we understand how to nurture the healing of others. Connect with me online and share your story. We will heal hearts and change the world.

CHAPTER SEVENTEEN

One Thousand Days of Gratitude

*"Gratitude changes lives,
one ripple at a time."*

ELDYKA SIMPSON

ELDYKA SIMPSON

Eldyka Simpson is a multi-faceted healer and entrepreneur whose eclectic mix of talents and tools have facilitated opportunities for deep healing and transformation in her patients, and led her to build Ripple Effect Wellness Centre in St. Albert, Alberta. Eldyka cares deeply, and approaches her work with a nurturing and intuitive spirit.

One part artist, Eldyka is a lifetime honorary member of the Ukrainian Shumka Dancers; one part healer, she incorporates acupuncture, massage therapy, craniosacral therapy, and energy healing into her clinic practice. A self-proclaimed birth warrior, Eldyka clawed her way out of a very deep postpartum depression via her one thousand-plus days of intentional (and very public) gratitude journaling.

Eldyka is a mother of four, grandmother of two, and wife to a man whom she has known since ninth grade. She loves being a dance and hockey mom and finds joy on the ball diamond, whether as her kids' biggest fan, team manager, or wannabe shortstop. She loves circling with her soulful sisters, discussing moon phases, the chakras, the power of nature, and partaking in sacred rituals and intuitively guided practices. Eldyka believes in a new paradigm of empowered birth, in building community and authentic connections, and in the innate goodness of people. She believes the Universe provides for each of us abundantly, and she believes strongly that we are all enough.

www.ripple-effect.ca
ig: @rippleeffectwellness_st.albert
fb: @rippleeffectwellnesscentre_st.albert

From my middle-class, suburban, white, privileged home in Edmonton, AB (on treaty six territory, traditional lands of First Nations and Métis people), it's easy to find things to be grateful for. I am blessed with a loving husband who has been my friend and my rock for more than half my life, four amazing children, two beautiful grandchildren, and a career that fills my heart and makes a difference to others. I am blessed to own my business and make enough money that we don't feel pinched anymore. For all intents and purposes, I can always find something to be thankful for. From this view, it's hard for me to admit that it wasn't always easy to be grateful. In fact, I would say I felt quite the opposite—resentful of all the people I care about, resentful of the work that lay before me; resentful that I, of all people, could find myself deep in the grasp of mental illness. I remember vividly, one day in early 2011, sitting in my vehicle at a traffic light with my infant son lovingly and safely strapped into his car seat behind me, and saying out loud, "Please, someone, just hit my car now." I never recall wanting to die, and I certainly didn't want anything to harm my little one. Looking back at that moment, which is permanently etched into my memory, I know that I wanted to be hurt enough that I would be admitted into the hospital, and that my responsibility to the world would be put on hold, at least for a little while.

Ever since I was a young girl, I have made it my life mission to care for others. I value the opportunity to be helpful, and I strive to create community and understanding in all situations. I am a *connector* and a *nurturer*, and it is from this place of heart-centeredness that I operate most authentically. It was no surprise that my career eventually turned toward caring for others as an RMT, acupuncturist, doula, and pregnancy empowerment guide. My strength as a practitioner and healer is that *I care deeply,* and the moment I declared that in a coaching and branding session back in 2015, everything about my business, Ripple Effect Wellness Centre, developed around this core tenet.

But at that moment at the stoplight, the last thing I wanted was to care for others. I had spent a lifetime doing it, and in that postpartum state of too little sleep, too little support, too much laundry, and too much time feeling very much alone despite being surrounded by three children under five (and a teenager to boot), I didn't want to care anymore.

I quickly realized no one was going to crash into me. I don't know if that realization caused me to spiral deeper or if it was the moment that I finally gave myself permission to spiral. Cue the dark, watery hell that is postpartum depression (PPD). It would be nearly three years before I clawed my way back.

I think anyone who has lived with PPD will have their own description of what it is for them. For me, it was a place of utter darkness, cold loneliness, and piercing self-judgment. It was a place where I was convinced no one could possibly understand how I felt, where I believed that our difficult breastfeeding journey was all my fault because who could be nourished by such a terrible example of a mother, and where my anger and rage came out at my family regularly, and grumpy mommy was the badge I donned daily.

Physically, I found myself in a perpetual state of exhaustion. I see now that my hormone levels were swinging wildly, bringing about extremely painful periods and terrifying mood swings, that punctuated both ovulation and the premenstrual period. I felt isolated and was terrified of the stigma surrounding mental illness and of how it would affect how others saw me. I stayed silent because I couldn't bear letting anyone down. I told no one how deeply I was hurting.

If I admit to having postpartum depression,
I mustn't love my babies.
If I actually do have PPD,
I must be a terrible mother.
If I have supported many women in my career
through their own bouts with PPD
yet can't cure myself,
I must also be a terrible acupuncturist.
And wow . . . who am I if I don't care for others
as a practitioner and a mom?
I must be nobody.

These thoughts and feelings ran deep through my veins during the months and years that followed. I remained silent for a long time. I knew at that time that I wouldn't find support from some of the family members closest to me, thanks to an old draconian belief that mental health issues were *in the head* (*well duh, it's their brain; that's in their head*). Clearly there was no need to look for support there.

I couldn't let go of the persona that I was a mother who had her shit together, so I wasn't honest about it with even my closest friends and clients. Truthfully, for a long time, I denied it even within myself, even though I knew for certain I had slipped into the realm of PPD. I believed it couldn't happen to me.

I suffered mostly in silence, and the stubborn acupuncturist in me never sought Western medical support. I see now that there is much benefit to a collaborative approach between allopathic and holistic medicines, but at that point, I had never really given much credit to pharmaceuticals or even doctors.

Luckily, in the previous decade, I had developed a network of amazing holistic practitioners from whom I received professional referrals and to whom I could refer my own patients. When I returned to work far sooner than the twelve-to-eighteen months granted through maternity leave now, one of these practitioners truly saw me, recognized the dark state I was in, and made time for my story. Sabrina offered care that encompassed healing of the mind, body, and spirit. Her treatments were not just about sticking needles into the right acupuncture points; they were infused with a deep love that I had never received from a practitioner before. (Undoubtedly, her treatments changed the way I approach my own patients now, and I'm forever grateful for her care during that difficult time.)

I saw a naturopath and an herbalist whose suggestions also helped get the hormonal imbalances under lasting control. I worked with an energy worker, who encouraged me to work through the energetic blockages and the emotional parts of my illness in a safe, sacred, and supported way.

At some point in all of this, I stumbled upon a daily gratitude journal written by an acquaintance named Arlene. I read anonymously for a while and decided in November 2012 that I would start my gratitude project as a sort of New Year's resolution. I laugh now at the ludicrousy of waiting over six weeks for a specific date to begin, but many things I did and believed during that time with PPD make me shake my head now.

"January 1, 2013. Day 1. I am grateful for having a chance to play with my kids during the holidays; for having my Mom in town for the holidays too, which was unexpected; and for going to work tomorrow for a little break from the chaos of cooped-up kids."

Some days, it was easy to find a few things to share, but on other days, especially in the early days, I had to push myself to find even one good thing. Those entries often used humor and any possible attempt to "spin" the day . . .

"Day 38. Today I'm grateful for the knowledge that when I ask the Universe for something, it listens . . . just a couple weeks ago I mentioned I could use a week off . . . just didn't expect I'd be sick when that week off arrived . . . sooo much snot . . . grateful for the chance to get my request clearer next time."

Or

"Day 154. Grateful . . . for kids who love me so much that bedtime took over ninety minutes, and was complete with a 'you're the

188

worst mommy ever' followed by a pleading 'please snuggle with me and stay until I fall asleep'."

Some days, my post was nothing more than a re-telling of my day, of the craziness of the life we had created with four kids, a business to run, a household to inspire, a world to change.

Over the next thousand days, my gratitude project brought me back to living my life intentionally. This single intentional act of being accountable to myself and my project every day forced me to become so much more present and aware of myself. It taught me how to shift my energies quickly from a place of disappointment and anger to one of acceptance and love.

My thousand days of gratitude took me from the lowest of lows to the highest of highs. They gave me an opportunity to find the beauty in the moments of sorrow and death:

"Day 59 . . . Tonight I am grateful for 38 years of love that I received from my Memere . . . summers spent in her garden and kneading dough, then baking the kid-sized buns in the lids of Mayonnaise jars . . . holidays and ordinary days where she offered the most beautiful blessings over our shared meals. And countless nights spent playing cards at her kitchen table . . . I'm grateful for the love she imbued with every cell of her being. I am so grateful that she was my grandmother. I will miss her so very much."

And to share the incredible honoring moment when the world is changed by a baby's birth:

"Day 982. For the magic of home births. For the perfectly-timed nudge that whispered, 'call the midwife' when it didn't seem like it was time . . . for the opportunity to bear witness to the strength of the human spirit and to the strength of the female body in all her glory."

I think I started the project to become aware of the goodness in my life, and perhaps to feel better as a parent. As I look back to some of my old posts, I know that the practice indeed helped affirm that I am doing well as a parent:

"Day 123. Grateful for my six-year-old daughter who doesn't even question two girls falling in love because as she said, 'it doesn't matter who someone loves'."

I know for certain my daily posts gave me the encouragement to find the resolve to try again after a particularly difficult day:

"Day 939. Grateful for the daily evening reminder on my phone that reminds me to aim for a gentle loving bedtime with the kids, but I got it too late tonight . . . and bedtime was a struggle because Mommy was a wee bit grumpy . . . tomorrow is a new day and we will try again."

My daily commitment to gratitude reminded me of the goodness in life and allowed me to share moments of absolute joy:

"Day 686. Grateful for much today, but none so much as the joyful, awesome, and peaceful news that my dear sweet friend Christina is free of cancer. 'Remission' is such a beautiful word."

My daily commitment to gratitude provided me opportunities to share moments of authentic connection and moments of awe:

"Day 924. Grateful for smiles that light up a person's entire being . . . you know the ones that start with a crinkle at the side of the eyes, an entire mouth engaging in a beautiful upward lift, and then actually infiltrating a whole body, open, relaxed, and ready to embrace that which has his attention . . . yes, grateful for those smiles."

"Day 947. Grateful tonight . . . for the most incredible sunset I've seen in awhile. Truly God kissed the sky this evening . . ."

My daily commitment to gratitude allowed me to share the growth of Ripple Effect Wellness Centre, from the very beginning all the way to the heart-led, award-winning powerhouse that it is:

"Day 973. I sit here this morning, in complete peace and reflection, and in sweet utter gratitude . . . There is absolutely no coincidence that it was in a circle of power-full, beauty-full, magical women that I birthed this 'business baby' this weekend . . . I am so blessed, and so deeply, deeply grateful."

I intended my gratitude practice to last for one month, but at the end of that time, it didn't feel complete, so I aimed for one hundred days. Then it just seemed right that I'd write for one year. But it continued, and for some strange, incredible reason, people kept reading. So I kept writing, motivated some days by the comments others would share with me, and motivated on other days by the fact that I couldn't possibly finish my gratitude posts on a "shitty day." (Reminder to self: quit nothing on a shitty day.)

"DAY 1000 . . . There were many days at the beginning of this project where I had trouble finding even one thing to be grateful for, and I . . . clung to the hope that each tomorrow would be a new day and would bring with it, more to be grateful for. And you know what? It ALWAYS did.

Little by little, I opened up to receiving more things to be grateful for . . . and I manifested incredible opportunities to reflect, and grow, and be awed. Little by little, I've managed to pull myself through some dark and lonely times, and find myself on the precipice of an incredibly inspiring adventure of living at my Highest Vibration. An adventure of living in Flow and Ease. An adventure of living in Abundance."

I've learned that Gratitude begets abundance—and I am abundant . . . I am blessed beyond measure and words for all the beauty-full, sacred, and soul-full people and opportunities that have come my way, paving the path for even more.

My one thousand days of gratitude have changed me. I am slowly but surely stepping into the person I have always meant to be . . . I AM ENOUGH.

My one thousand days of gratitude have changed me. I am not sure where the path will lead me, but . . . I am confident . . . that my Soul has agreed to every twist and turn along the way.

My one thousand days of gratitude have changed me. I now know within my heart that it is my Soul's purpose to care deeply, and to nurture and to forge deep connections. Everything I do must be done from this point of authenticity, and everything must be done with Love. For it is when I share my true authentic self that I make a difference.

And in the end, we are all here to make a difference.

So on this one thousandth day, I am grateful to Pacha Mama, Mother Earth, Spirit, and God—for as I learn to open myself up to your never-ending support, I know deep within myself that I can never go wrong.

I am grateful for everyone who has nurtured, inspired and reached out to me, who has made me laugh from my deep center, who has invited me to grow . . .

Day one thousand. I am grateful."

Over the course of one thousand days, I became acutely aware of how my mindset and my life were changing. I got curious about the science behind gratitude and found a beautiful abundance of research extolling its benefits.

In a white paper prepared for the John Templeton Foundation by the GGSC entitled "The Science of Gratitude," it was reported that those who regularly shared gratitude have signs of better psychological health, including higher levels of perceived social support and lower levels of stress, depression, and anxiety.[1] Gratitude expert Robert Emmons further reported that those who regularly express gratitude have stronger immune systems, increased psychological well-being, and more positive relationships overall.

---

1   Allen, Summer, P.h.D. 2018. *The Science of Gratitude.* Greater Good Science Center (GGSC), UC Berkley. Retrieved from https://ggsc.berkeley.edu/images/uploads/GGSC-JTF_White_Paper-Gratitude-FINAL.pdf

One of the most remarkable pieces of research that I found, an essay published by the Greater Good Science Center (GGSC)[2], noted that simply thinking about being grateful sparks the same chemical cascade within the brain as when you are actually feeling grateful. In his book *Upward Spiral,* Dr. Alex Korb states, " . . . trying to think of things you are grateful for . . . increases serotonin production."[3] This means that even if you can't find something to be grateful for, your brain changes regardless, and you may see improvements in sleep, mood regulation, and metabolism . . . how cool is that?!

Melody Beattie says, *"Gratitude makes sense of our past, brings peace for today, and creates a vision for tomorrow."*[4]

Indeed, my gratitude project did all of these things for me. It helped me move through my depression in due time. It brought me an incredible sense of peace for the life I have chosen and the life I am creating. As I have healed, gratitude has continued to guide me every step of the way. In my work today, I often recommend a gratitude practice to my patients as a way to support their healing and to promote growth and transformation. Gratitude is an easy practice on the surface, but the practice of daily gratitude requires commitment to see long-lasting change. While I won't ever suggest that a gratitude project needs to be public in order to hold the most benefits, I do recommend finding a way to keep yourself accountable.

I am several years beyond my postpartum battle now, and I have intimate knowledge of how burn-out, disconnection, and a society that praises the multi-tasker can bring even the strongest of us down. I eventually realized that I couldn't remain silent about my history with PPD. My work at Ripple Effect Wellness Centre is largely with moms in whom I see my younger self, struggling to keep their identity clear, their kids in check, and their families glued together. I recognize now that in sharing my story, I give others permission to share their own. I recognize all of us need to be seen, need to be loved, and need to be cared for deeply.

2   Wong, Joel. Brown, Joshua. 2017. How Gratitude Changes You and Your Brain. *The Science of Gratitude.* Greater Good Science Center (GGSC), UC Berkley. Retrieved from https://greatergood.berkeley.edu/article/item/how_gratitude_changes_you_and_your_brain
3   Korb, Alex. 2015. *The Upward Spiral.* Oakland: New Harbinger Publications.
4   Beattie, Melody. 2017 "Gratitude." Accessed January 18, 2020. https://melodybeattie.com/gratitude-2/

I am so grateful for the lessons that have brought me here. That moment at the stoplight is a distant memory now, and I am so grateful to be back in a space where I want to care deeply again. Thank you for holding space for my story. I am so very grateful for you.

GUIDED MEDITATION

Jennifer Jayde

Hello Beautiful Soul,

It is I, your highest self communicating to you through the open channel created by Jennifer Jayde, at the request of the beautiful co-authors of this book who deeply love and support you. Feel us wrapping you up now in a blanket of complete and unconditional love, light, and warmth.

I am here to remind you that you are not alone. You never were, and you never will be.

You are an old soul who signed up for the Masterclass Life Experience, which is not for the faint of heart.

This is how I know you are strong, because you chose big bold experiences for this life.

Now it is important that you breathe through, let go, and release the energy of the old—to make room for the new. New opportunities of strength, exhilaration, freedom and joy—for yourself, and those around you. New opportunities of purpose, inspiration and empowerment are available to you now.

As we breathe, we exchange draining, heavy energy, for a powerful cleansing flow of divine light energy throughout our entire being. It's the difference between feeling like a murky stagnant swamp, or a fresh flowing river of crystal clear water from within.

Breath means "Spirit" and breathing is the act of bringing more Spirit energy from Source, down into your physical body. It is both healing and freeing for you (and as a result) all those around you who's lives you impact and inspire.

Are you ready to set yourself free?
Then let's begin…

1. Close your eyes and become more aware of your physical body. Notice your toes and whether or not they are relaxed, then your calves, your quads, and all the way up the rest of your body, one area at a time. Sink deeply back into the chair or couch or bed you are on. Let it all go, even for just these few minutes.

2. Coming home to your breath, I invite you to practise four box breaths, *(which is something you can do anytime you're feeling any kind of worry or anxiety in your life)* by inhaling slowly for the count of four, holding for four, exhaling for four, holding for four. Repeat four times.

3. Envision a beam of light coming out of your crown chakra *(the top of your head)* all the way up and up and up, through the ceiling, through the sky, through the stars. Keep going past all the other planets and galaxies, until you see a bright, pearly, iridescent light above you. Enter this light. You are connected to Source.

4. Here you are free to ask for whatever you'd like. You are limitless. You may call upon deceased friends and family to surround you with love and light. You may hug them, and receive their encouragement and strength. You may ask to fill every cell of your body with the pureness, power, and cleansing strength of the divine. Breathe this positive empowering experience into every fibre of your being, inside your body and outside through your aura. Take as much time as you need.

5. Travel back down the tunnel of light, back down passed the stars and the planets, through the sky, through the ceiling and back home into your body.

6. Feel the tunnel of light follow you down from source, and wash through you like a rushing waterfall shower from the divine, cleansing your thoughts, your mind, each of your chakras, every cell in your body, your aura, and going right through you down into mother earth. Anything that no longer serves you has been washed down into the core of Mother Earth so that she may neutralize and recycle this energy to become cleansed and useful again.

When you're ready, slowly wiggle your fingers and toes, bringing your conscious awareness back into your body, and the present moment. Take a final deep cleansing, healing breathe—until you are feeling awake, vibrant, refreshed and alive.

You are strong. You are free....

To listen to an audio extended version of this meditation to guide you in real time, head to *www.jenniferjayde.com/meditation*

Jennifer Jayde is a Soul Aligned Success Coach for women who desire to inspire, using their life experience to empower others. She is an internationally, two time bestselling and two time award winning Author/Speaker/Coach, and creator of the highly sought after Awakener's Certification. Born and raised in Canada into humble beginnings, she's now been featured in notable magazines, interviews and podcasts internationally, appeared on television in both Canada and the USA, and spoken in front of many captivated audiences. She's also the host of the popular spiritual growth podcast: The Soul Adventurer, and her most recent best selling book, *The Awakening - A Guide to Spiritually Awaken Your Highest Self, Intuitive Connection, and Deepest Purpose*—is available worldwide on Amazon now. Jennifer resides with her hubby part-time on Vancouver Island, Canada, and part-time in San Diego California.

RESOURCE GUIDE

A

- Association of Alberta Sexual Assault Services (AASAA) | Alberta, Canada | www.aasas.ca

C

- Canada Drug Rehab Addiction Services Directory | Canada | 1-866-462-6362
- Canadian Women's Foundation | Toronto, ON, Canada | www.canadianwomen.org | 1-866-293-4483
- Canadian Women's Foundation | Calgary, AB, Canada | www.canadianwomen.org | 1-403-984-2523
- COAST: Crisis Outreach and Support Team | check out your local COAST helpline | Niagara, ON region | 1-866-550-5205
- Crisis Services Canada | Canada | 1-833-456-4566 | Text 45645

D

- Dandelion Society | Victoria, BC, Canada | www.hopeliveshere.ca/find-help
- Destiny Rescue: Ending Child Trafficking and Sexual Exploitation | Australia, New Zealand & USA | www.destinyrescue.org
- Doctor Ramani: Narcissism Expert, Licensed Clinical Psychologist, Best-Selling Author, Professor of Psychology, Distinguished Speaker, & Workplace | New Jersey, USA | www.doctor-ramani.com
- Domestic Shelters | Canada & USA | www.domesticshelters.org/

E

- Ending Violence, Association of Canada | Canada | www.endingviolencecanada.org/getting-help/

F

- First Nations and Inuit Hope for Wellness Help Line | Canada | 1-855-242-3310

G

- Greater VICTORIA Victim Services | Victoria, BC, Canada | https://www.gvpvs.org/

J

- Jennifer Summerfeldt, MACP; CCC: Trauma-Informed Psychotherapy | Edmonton, AB, Canada | In-person and Online | www.jennifersummerfeldt.com | 780-902-6264

K

- Kids Help Phone | 1-800-668-6868

N

- National Eating Disorder Information Centre (NEDIC) | USA | 1-866-633-4220
- Native Youth Crisis Hotline | Canada & USA | https://crisiscentre.bc.ca/fnha/ | 1-877-209-1266

O

- Ontario Network of Sexual Assault/Domestic Violence Treatment Centres | Ontario, Canada https://www.sadvetreatmentcentres.ca

R

- Recovery: An American Addiction Centers Resource | USA | www.recovery.org/addiction/domestic-violence

S

- Shelters:

  Canada | www.sheltersafe.ca
  Canada & USA | www.domesticshelters.org
  UK | www.refuge.org.uk
  USA | www.womenshelters.org

V

- Victim Services | Canada | www.justice.gc.ca/eng/cj-jp/victims-victimes/vsd-rsv/index.html
- Victoria Women's Transition House | Victoria, BC, Canada | www.transitionhouse.net
- Voice Found: prevention of child sexual abuse and trafficking | www.voicefound.ca

W

- Women Against Violence | Duncan, BC, Canada | www.cwav.org/our_services | 250-748-8544 250.748.8544
- Womens College Hospital | Toronto, ON, Canada | www.womenscollegehospital.ca

ACKNOWLEDGMENTS

"To my amazing family, I am forever grateful for your love and support. You helped me through my illness, and my day-to-day life. I love you all to the moon and back, to the stars and beyond."

-Katryna Rose

"To Stephen. Thank you for always encouraging me to be my best self. To my family: Ann, Les, and Elaine. Thank you for your unconditional love and support no matter what."

-Nicole Thomas

"To my mom, you are the strength behind me. To my husband for giving me space to share this story. To my dad, through you I learned grit and tenacity."

-Nicole Taylor Eby

"I love you, Mom. Thank you for my lifesavers: God, Drew, Paul, Janette, and all of those who walked with me. To my students: you are loved and can do anything. Even write a book!"

-Cassaundra Noyes

"Special thanks to my love Vincent, who pushed me to share my story in this book project, and for his help that makes me grow every single day by his side. I love you."

-Violaine Pigeon

"Thank you God for giving me life and faith. To my sweet Rene for your love, my friends for your support, and Yvonne for your encouragement. To Kate, Jackie, Bill, Shawn, Kelly, and Dr. David Cree, you twinkle as lights in the darkest of skies."

-Lori Williamson

"I dedicate these words to all those who think they are alone and unworthy of joy and love. YOU ARE NOT ALONE."

-Charleyne Oulton (Charley)

"I'd like to thank my family and friends for their unwavering love and support. I couldn't have gotten this far without it. Also, Lori Beneteau Photography for the photo to accompany this chapter."

-Lindsay Whitham

"To my mother, I miss you more every day. To my father, thank you for your never-ending love and support. To Victoria, I will cherish your friendship always. To Dave, thank you for never giving up on me."

-Mlle Elizabeth Ann

"To my mother, you have been my stable heart and home throughout this journey into motherhood. Without you, I feel our lives would be very different. You are our safe space."

-Sasha Rose

"To my husband Don and my daughters, Mika and Keaton, you held my hand, held me up, and helped my laugh through the tears."

-Stephanie Reid

"My heartfelt gratitude to my children, husband, and Daddy; your ongoing love, care, understanding, and encouragement has supported me as I heal and share my truths. To the numerous others who have been a light in my journey, thank you."

-Angel Kibble

"Thank you to everyone who saw the real me during the times I had lost her. The friends who are now family, my coaches who are my rocks, and the strong, inspiring women who made this book a reality."

-Kady Romagnuolo

"To the brave and brilliant authors, speakers, and humans I have had the honor of interacting with, knowing and learning from. Thank you for sharing your truths, your stories, and for tearing me from my isolation."

-Mandy Karpoff

"To Ryan, who made the phone call when I couldn't."

-Kiki Carr

"Blessings to the souls who signed up to support me on my journey this lifetime."

-Whitney Stout

"To Sabrina, you offered me the deepest love in any acupuncture treatment and changed my path as a practitioner. To my beloved Russ and my incredible children, your unconditional love gives me a soft place to land as I chase my lofty dreams."

-Eldyka Simpson

GOLDEN BRICK ROAD
PUBLISHING HOUSE

Link arms with us as we pave new paths to a better and more expansive world.

Golden Brick Road Publishing House (GBRPH) is a small, independently initiated boutique press created to provide social-innovation entrepreneurs, experts, and leaders a space in which they can develop their writing skills and content to reach existing audiences as well as new readers.

Serving an ambitious catalogue of books by individual authors, GBRPH also boasts a unique co-author program that capitalizes on the concept of "many hands make light work." GBRPH works with our authors as partners. Thanks to the value, originality, and fresh ideas we provide our readers, GBRPH books are now available in bookstores across North America.

We aim to develop content that effects positive social change while empowering and educating our members to help them strengthen themselves and the services they provide to their clients.

Iconoclastic, ambitious, and set to enable social innovation, GBRPH is helping our writers/partners make cultural change one book at a time.

Inquire today at www.goldenbrickroad.pub